The Industrial L[egacy] Landscapes

Sheffield and South Yorkshire

Sheffield Hallam University

Landscape, Archaeology and Ecology
Special Series No.4

Edited by Ian D. Rotherham and Christine Handley

ISBN: 978-1-904098-67-6

September 2017

Published by:
Wildtrack Publishing, Venture House,
103 Arundel Street, Sheffield S1 2NT

Supported by:

PLACE (People, Landscape & Cultural Environment of Yorkshire)
South Yorkshire Biodiversity Research Group
HEC Associates
Landscape Conservation Forum
Sheffield Hallam University

© Wildtrack Publishing and the individual authors 2017

All rights reserved. No part of this publication may be reproduced or transmitted in any form or by any means, electronic or mechanical, including photocopying, recording, or any information storage or retrieval system, without permission in writing from the publisher.

Front cover: Postcard - White Rails, River Don, Sheffield by Hayward Young in the early 1900s

Contents

Foreword 1

The Industrial transformation of South Yorkshire landscapes
Ian D. Rotherham
.... 3

Regulating a Pre-Modern, Industrial, Urban Landscape: Street Cleaning, Waste-disposal and Insanitary Nuisances in Sheffield, 1500-1700
Leona Skelton
.... 41

The Wentworth-Fitzwilliams of Wentworth Woodhouse: Industrial Entrepreneurs for Three Centuries
Melvyn Jones
..…... 57

Snuff and Grouse: The Wilsons of Sharrow
David Hey.
.... 81

The Industrial Legacy & Landscapes of Sheffield and South Yorkshire

Barker's Pool Sheffield in the 1700s

Foreword

This volume of papers arose from the 1-day conference *The Industrial Legacy & Landscapes of Sheffield and South Yorkhire* that was held in Sheffield. It was organised by South Yorkshire Biodiversity Research Group with PLACE (People, Landscape & Cultural Environment) based in York and with Sheffield Hallam University.

The conference included presentations in the morning and early afternoon followed by guided walks around the central part of Sheffield looking at evidence of landscape change and industrial impacts. There were two walks, one looking at the eighteenth century industrial area and city centre and another along the banks of the River Don that not only showed the nineteenth century developments but also evidence of the medieval town.

The topics reflected some of the breadth and variety in both the landscapes and the industrial legacies that can be seen across South Yorkshire and around Sheffield in particular. The volume includes chapters by several of the speakers including Professor David Hey who sadly passed away a few months after the conference took place. This book is dedicated to his memory.

Dedicated to Professor David Hey
(1938-2016)

The Industrial transformation of South Yorkshire landscapes

Ian D. Rotherham
Sheffield Hallam University

> *'Don, like a weltering worm, lies blue below,*
> *And Wincobank, before me, rising green,*
> *Calls from the South the silvery Rother slow,*
> *And smile on moors beyond, and meads between,*
> *Unrivall'd landscape'* Ebenezer Elliot, 1836

Figure 1: White Rails, River Don, Sheffield by Hayward Young in the early 1900s

Summary

Sheffield is the main city within the greater South Yorkshire region. With a long history of industrial development, mineral coal mining and steel manufacture, this was a world leader of the Industrial Revolution. However, during the 1970s, there began a dramatic downturn in the industrial economy, leaving a legacy of environmental pollution and land degradation, and a history of chronic ill-health associated with industrial disease. A period of rapid transformation, of major political unrest and industrial strike action, and the closure of many traditional industries and their factories followed. Unemployment grew to around 20% of the working population and both social and environmental problems grew. In response to this challenging situation regional stakeholders – business, politicians, workers and the community, began to adapt to the new circumstances.

A long process of environmental recovery and restoration began in order to both re-cycle derelict lands to make them available for new development, and importantly to change the poor perceptions of the region. Critical steps with both planning and management interventions undertaken to facilitate the processes of recovery. This paper reviews actions, initiatives and impacts and considers their transferability to other regions. In particular, there was a sequential process of 'cleaning and greening' and re-branding, of re-structuring critical infrastructure, and then through major intervention, the kick starting of a new economy through sports mega events, leisure retail, and entertainments. The research approach entails a long-term observational study and triple bottom line evaluations of economic, social and environmental impacts.

Urbanisation and industry transformed landscapes and environments across the city region, both directly and indirectly. At the heart of the process was the historic River Don, which provided a focus for the first coordinated actions to renew and regenerate the Valley. In 2007, the consequences of centuries of human impacts on the watercourse and its wider catchment became obvious as the region was subjected to the worst floods ever records here. However, today the river is ecologically renewed. It has re-emerged as a vital living artery for the City linking people, nature, and place. The evidence of the timelines of historic change is still visible today.

Figure 2: Work-a-day Sheffield by Hayward Young of the River Don and Blonk Bridge in the early 1900s

Introduction

Sheffield and its hinterland of South Yorkshire are located in to the north of the English Midlands. A major river system, the Don to the Humber, flows to the east and out to the North Sea, and the high ground of the Peak District National Park is to the west. Until the 1600s or 1700s, this was largely an ancient landscape of wetlands, rivers, moors, commons, woods and forests, and deer parks and chases (Bownes *et al.*, 1991; Rotherham, 2010). There was some localised industry linked to early metalworking, coppice woodland management, and especially to waterpower from the rivers. Urban development was restricted to small riverside settlements of a few thousand people in Sheffield, Rotherham, Chesterfield, Barnsley and Doncaster. Some of these originated perhaps fifteen hundred years ago in Roman times.

From the early 1600s, Sheffield grew in under 200 years, from around 10,000 people to over 300,000 to become a capital of world industry covering around 300 square kilometres of varied landform. This growth centred on a series of river valleys and hills, and the area has over eighty ancient woods, extensive heather moorland and bog, together with urban relict grasslands, and remarkable post-industrial sites. The rivers and valleys running from the high western ground to the lowlands, act as the spokes of a wheel converging on the city centre. These provide a network of natural green corridors allowing the persistence of semi-natural wildlife areas into the heart of the city.

This chapter describes the long-term transformation of a region and its main city. Through industrialisation and urbanisation, over a period of around 500 years, Sheffield and South Yorkshire changed from primarily rural, to massively industrial, and then in the late twentieth century to post-industrial. The recent drivers of change have included post-industrial urban renewal with the catalysts of sport, leisure, tourism, education and environment. These have combined to transform both places and people.

The case study is based on Sheffield, England, the city lying within the greater South Yorkshire region. A world leader of the Industrial Revolution, it has a long history of industrial development, mineral coal mining and steel manufacture. However, during the 1970s, there began a dramatic downturn in the industrial economy, leaving a legacy of environmental pollution and land degradation, and a history of chronic ill-health associated with industrial disease.

Figure 3: Sheffield soots you

Decline was followed by a period of rapid transformation, of major political unrest and industrial strike action, and the closure of many traditional industries and their factories. Unemployment grew to around 20% of the working population and both social and environmental problems grew. In response to this challenging situation regional stakeholders – business, politicians, workers and the community, began to adapt to the new circumstances. A long process of environmental recovery and restoration began in order to both re-cycle derelict lands to make them available for new development, and importantly to change the poor perceptions of the region. Some critical steps were taken to facilitate the processes of recovery and these are described later. The broad situation was described in my book, 'Lost Sheffield in Colour', and this neatly summarises Sheffield in the early to mid, twentieth century (Rotherham, 2013c):

'Sheffield is the fourth largest city in England, and despite its history of steel, iron, coal and manufacturing, boasts more ancient woodlands than any other industrial centre in Western Europe. It is a remarkable place with unique heritage and deep-seated contradictions in its character, its people and its heritage. Described by George Orwell in the *Road to Wigan Pier*, as the dirtiest, smelliest, ugliest city in the world, its name became a by-word for clean air.'

'...But even Wigan is beautiful compared with Sheffield. Sheffield, I suppose, could justly claim to be called the ugliest town in the Old World; its inhabitants. Who want it to be pre-eminent in everything, very likely do make that claim for it…… And the stench! If at rare moments you stop smelling sulphur it is because you have begun smelling gas. Even the shallow river that runs through the town is usually bright yellow with some chemical or other. Once, I halted in the street and counted the factory chimneys I could see; there were thirty-three of them, but there would have been far more if the air had not been obscured by smoke.'
George Orwell, 1937

Orwell goes on to point out that whilst there is no inherent reason why industry should be dirty and ugly, *'Northerners'* have become used to and tolerant of these conditions. Today, as Melvyn Jones points out, Sheffield is the most wooded industrial city in Western Europe. Poet Laureate John Betjeman praised the western suburbs of Sheffield as some of the greenest and prettiest in England. This is a part of the mixed up personality of Sheffield. The city, which led the Industrial Revolution, also gave rise to campaigns for access to the countryside and ultimately both National Parks and Green Belts. Sheffield was where the Industrial Revolution began in earnest and became the biggest steel manufacturing centre in Europe. The city's high-quality steels and fine cutlery were and still are, famous across the world. Today there are two large universities and at Meadowhall the biggest shopping centre in Europe, yet there is so much more to its history and its heritage. As a border town between north and south, from the Romans onwards, this region was significant in national politics and power. The great Saxon Kingdom of Northumbria extended from here north to Edinburgh, and to the south was Mercia, the powerhouse of a united English kingdom. The River Don divided the north from the south, a division reinforced by great wetlands and wooded areas of higher ground. To this day, Sheffield is a border town; the south of the north rather than the north of the south, and the lowland edge of the uplands, not *vice versa.*'

By 1843, the average age of people dying in the city centre was just twenty-four years with chronically poor public health and acute industrial diseases (Walton, 1948). Indeed, in the 1970s, I was still being encouraged by my school in Sheffield to pursue a career in medicine, and the university's medical school was highly recommended because of the interesting range of nasty industrial accidents and the unique industrial diseases.

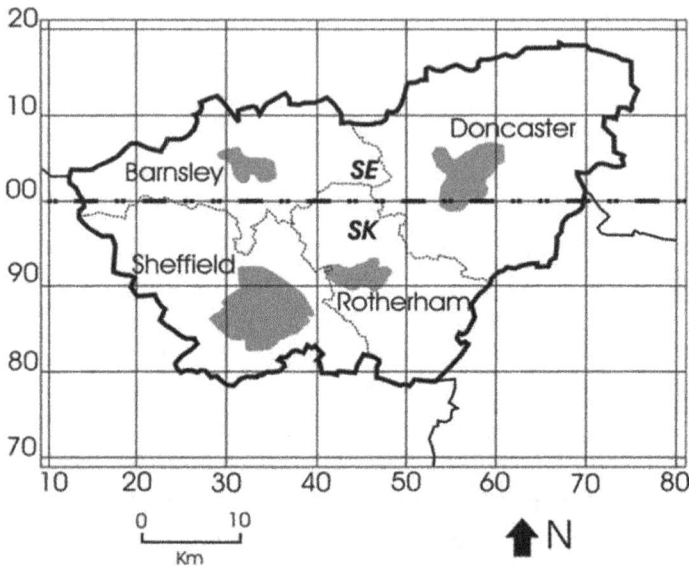

Figure 4: Sheffield in South Yorkshire

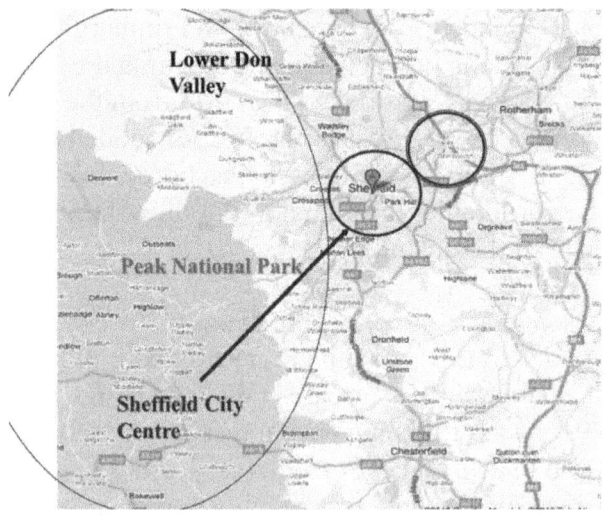

Figure 5: Sheffield and the Lower Don Valley in their wider context

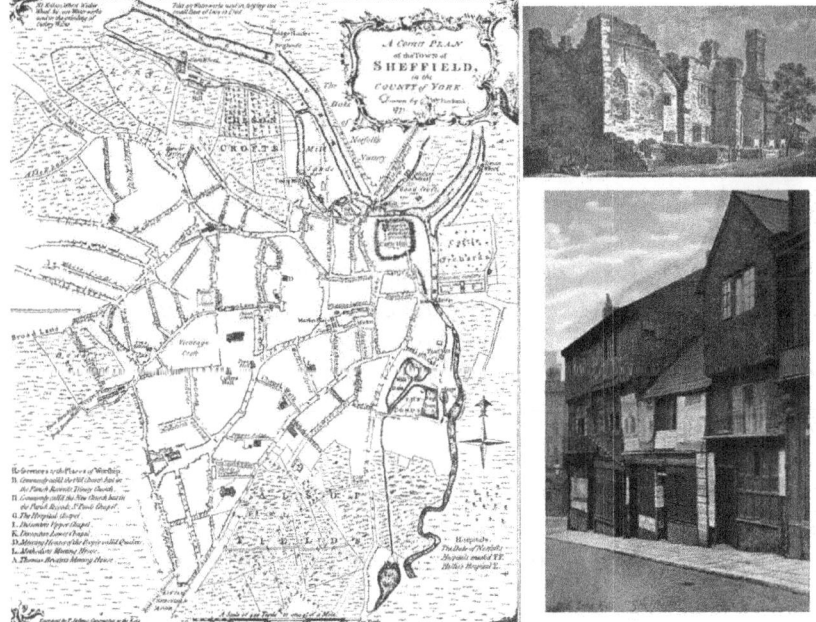

Figure 6: Sheffield in 1771

The Don: a river with history

In the early 1900s, a dugout canoe, now in Sheffield Museum, was found in sediments near Meadowhall; testimony to the wet prehistoric landscape of extensive wet alder and willow woodland, with meandering river channels, pools and marshes, the long-lost 'Lake Meadowhall'. Place-names such as Holmes Farm at Blackburn Meadows suggest an island settlement in a marsh. The Don is a river with 'attitude', and a tendency to flood but over time, people colonised the area and farming pushed back the water's edge. By medieval times, the river would have been lined by rich, productive waterside meadows and winter floodlands. These provided valuable summer grazing and hay crops, and marsh resources for basket making, peat fuel, reed thatch, fish and wildfowl.

In 1546, the ancient chapel at Attercliffe was still in use and the curate of Rotherham, the major town and main ecclesiastical centre, would come to his flock when it was too wet for them to come to him '…….. *to mynistre to the seke people, as when the waters of the Rothere and Downe* [DON] *are so urgent that the curate of Rotherham cannot to them repayre, nor the inhabitants unto hym nether on horseback or bote……*' (Hunter, 1819).

Along the Rivers Don and Rother, until the 1950s, many local people had boats in case the river burst its banks; all part of living near the water. The rivers, Don, Rother and Dearne, run from the western fringes of the Pennines through into the lowlands of South Yorkshire. For over two centuries, they have served as the arteries through both rural and industrial landscapes.

The Dearne Valley for example, was changed from medieval countryside and flood meadows to deep-mined coal, mostly during the mid-1800s to mid-1900s. The medieval settlements still stand out in the modern landscape and set back from the riverine floodplain.

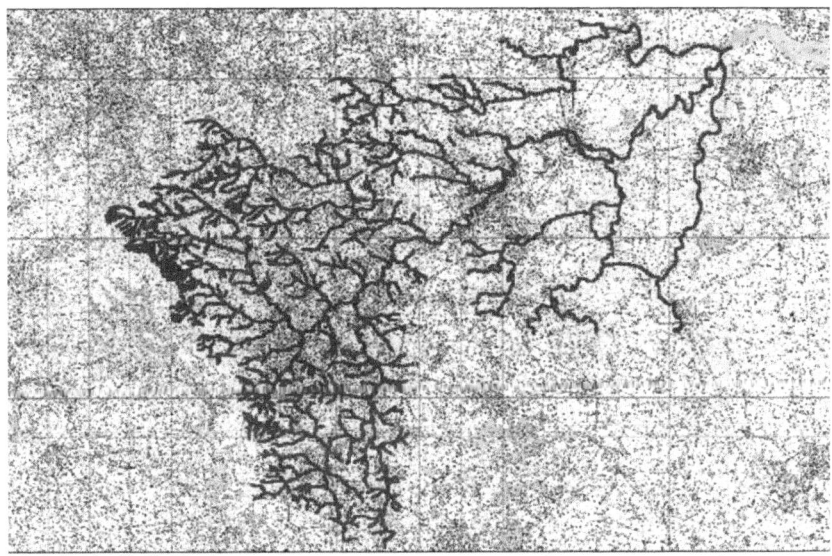

Modelled by Keith Harrison

Figure 7: The River Don catchment before industrialisation

Modelled by Keith Harrison

Figure 8: Dearne Valley floodlands

Figure 9: Wath Main Colliery in the 1950s

Figure 10: Twenty-first century dereliction

Oliver Rackham (1986) suggested that, 'about a quarter of the British Isles is, or has been, some kind of wetland', and Chris Smout (2001), stated, 'There are many thousands of hectares of what is now prime arable land, especially in northern England, that were in the 17th century, fen and mire'. Smout goes on, '...it is surprising how...Yorkshire.. fenlands have evaporated from general memory'.

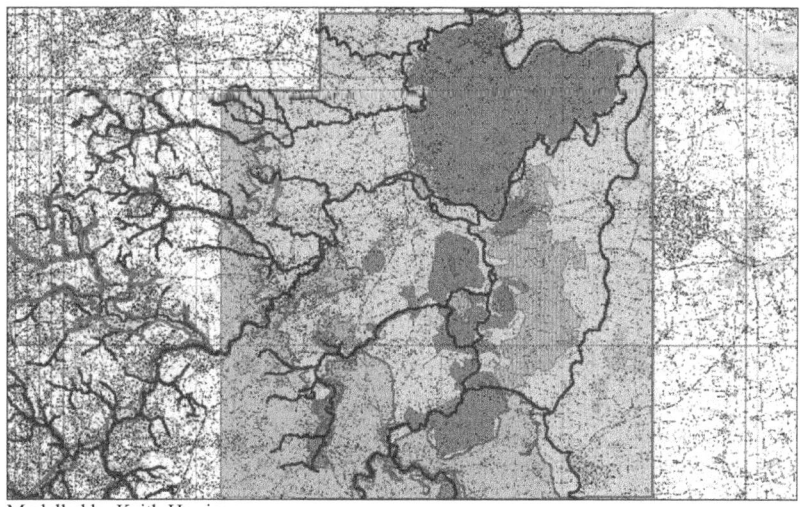

Modelled by Keith Harrison

Figure 11: The lower catchment and the extensive peatlands before transformation

In Yorkshire south of the confluence of the Ouse and the Trent, 70,000 acres of Hatfield Chase were constantly inundated before Vermuyden and his fellow Dutch undertakers commenced to drain it in 1626 (Rotherham, 2010). At its heart was Thorne Mere, almost a mile over, and close by, Potterick Carr with 4,000 acres near Doncaster, fell to Smeaton and his engineers after a private Act of Parliament in 1764. This was one of many outliers known as the Yorkshire Carrs. (See Rotherham, 2010 for more detail). Alongside the well-known transformation to industry of Sheffield city, these great wetlands were also industrialised (Rotherham & Cartwright, 2000, 2001):

'…..the moors have been developed in an extraordinary manner by the manipulation of the surface for peat moss litter which has now become a most important trade, the Thorne Moors finding employment for 350 hands in stripping the surface of the waste for litter. When the surface has been cleared, sluices made for the purpose are opened to admit the tidal water from the rivers Ouse and Don, which brings up rich earthy matter called 'warp' and deposits it on the land; by this treatment, pursued for about 3 years, extensive tracts of the waste have, since the beginning of the 19th century, been converted into fertile land of the most valuable kind.'
(Quoted in Goodchild, 1971 (see Rotherham, 2010))

Prior to transformation, these peatlands were dramatic and immense. Woodruffe-Peacock,1920-21, provides a description of the variation in volume and hence height with seasonal conditions, attributed to the very wet core of the bog.

'In rainy seasons …… its central mass was feet higher when full and swollen with water than in dry summers with normal rainfall, as it lifted as it swelled on the principle of in summer the dry and in winter the wet sponge. This I have over and over again observed personally from the great central Railway line, as in wet times nothing on its northern side was visible which could be clearly distinguished in dry summer weather. In 1875 it was estimated that the winter rise and summer fall of the bog was about six feet, in an abnormally wet season in the sixties, eight feet.'

Economies transformed

Much of this landscape was ecologically intact and provided a great natural resource for local people until maybe the 1700s. Then, with parliamentary enclosures of the countryside, rapid development of industry, and a dramatic growth in urban populations, the region was transformed.

The Agricultural Revolution displaced the common people from the rural lands and the Industrial Revolution in the cities sucked them in as wage slaves. This region was one of a number in England pivotal in triggering the rise of global industry, and for two hundred years Sheffield grew into the biggest steel manufacturing centre in Europe and one of the largest in the world. It was also the centre of deep mined mineral coal and especially famous for its cutlery with 'Made in Sheffield' becoming a hallmark for good quality.

THE TRANSFORMATION TO INDUSTRIAL CENTRE

Traditional, medieval, rural ⟶ Modern, industrial, urban

Figure 12: The process of transformation

People & communities transformed

Across the region, rural communities began a rapid transformation and a de-population. The poorer people and the less affluent peasants, who formerly subsisted in the countryside, became rural, often seasonal labour or unemployed. Many migrated to the cities and towns that in turn sprawled out across the once green landscapes. Towns such as Sheffield grew rapidly from a few thousand inhabitants in 1600 to hundreds of thousands of people by the 1800s. Growth was a mix of increased birth rates and inward migration. Although material conditions such as much of the housing was better in the town than the countryside, the situation rapidly deteriorated as services and provisions were overwhelmed. Indeed, by the 1800s the land, air and water were grossly polluted (e.g. Gilbertson *et al.*, 1997), and mortality in the urban centres grew alarmingly (Walton, 1948).

Air pollution took its toll in bronchial diseases and these were exacerbated by exposure to metallic wastes and dusts inhaled in the cramped confined spaces of urban industrial sweatshops. By the 1970s, Sheffield University medical School was the place to study if you wanted to gain experience in nasty industrial diseases from metalworking or mining, or in serious industrial accidents. Along with air pollution, the towns' water supplies were also a source of disease and death as cholera and typhoid took their toll. By the mid 1800s, the average life expectancy in inner city Sheffield was around twenty years. The brand of 'Made in Sheffield' came at a cost in human life and suffering (Walton, 1948; Williamson, 1990).

Landscapes transformed

Farmland was changed from communal use to private estates and their individual farmsteads. Rivers were straightened and canalised, wetlands and moors were drained, and woods were felled or put into intensive industrial coppice management – to produce vital charcoal for iron and steel making. Ancient deer parks were sacrificed in order to extract metals and minerals from the land below them. Around the expanding urban centres, farms were managed to produce the vital and staple foods demanded by a rapidly growing town population. The footprint of the urban extended into and throughout the rural hinterland. In the urban heartlands air pollution masked the landscape for six days of the week, and only on Sunday did the veil lift and the greenery reappear for a brief respite.

A powerhouse for the world & the empire

Sheffield and its region was a powerhouse not only for England, but also for the world beyond (Walton, 1948; Lawless, 1990; Watts *et al.*, 1987). As the British Empire spread around the planet, materials manufactured and produced here spread as a global brand. This reached a peak in the mid twentieth century as a slow decline began in the aftermath of the Second World War. However, the emerging city was not just an industrial centre, and as an economic hub it drew in and nurtured academics and philosophers, writers, artists, industrialists, inventors, and politicians. From the energy of industry grew an engine of social and educational development and reform. Yet this emergence was in the face of a rapid decline in social welfare, in health and in quality of life for the vast majority of people. The other major cost was in the almost total decline in environmental quality as rivers once rich in salmon and other fish became dead stinking sewers. Riverside pastures and meadows were destroyed or grossly polluted (Watts *et al.*, 1987; Rotherham & Cartwright, 2000, 2001).

Political & social transformation

In the midst of huge social tensions, of massive gaps between rich and poor, and of enormous dysfunction in ecosystems and political systems, there emerged a rich vein of intellectual debate and radical thinking. Sheffield the industrial city built on steel became a furnace for cultural change as a new society grew from the smogs and slums of economic exploitation. Ideas emerged on:

- **Social housing**
- **Public parks and green spaces**
- **Civic open spaces**
- **National Parks and access to the countryside**
- **Green Belts to limit urban sprawl**
- **Libraries and art galleries**
- **Workers education and self-improvement**
- **Health and welfare**
- **Religion and especially non-conformism**

Transportation transformed

In the 1700s in England, transport by any means was notoriously difficult. But by the mid 1700s rivers and new canals provided effective transportation for industrial raw materials and for manufactured products for export. From Sheffield a network of newly built canals and engineered rivers spread far and wide and water transport led from the urban industrial centres to the coastal ports. However, sooner after the canals were completed, in the 1800s, steam-powered railways fuelled by locally dug coal usurped them. Over the centuries from the 1500s onwards, a series of major transportation transformations occurred across the region:

- Packhorse and carriage 1500s
- Turnpikes (toll-roads) 1700s
- Canals 1700s
- Macadam roads 1700s / 1800s
- Railways 1800s
- Electric trams 1900s
- Tarmac roads 1800s
- Motorways 1960s
- Airports 1980s / 1990s
- Supertram 1990s
- Cycleways 1990s
- Upgraded road networks 1990s
- High Speed Railway electrification 2010+, and controversially perhaps, HS2

The late twentieth century & industrial decline

From the 1970s into the 1990s, the city and region entered a rapid and dramatic downturn in its industrial base. Furthermore, whilst a reorganised specialist steel sector continued to thrive, it now employed relatively small numbers of people. At the start of the 1970s, the industrial Lower Don Valley in Sheffield employed around 70,000 people directly and many more in related service industries. Most of these people lived in tightly packed communities in and around the valley where they worked. Almost overnight, the jobs and the people had gone for ever (Lawless, 1990; Watts *et al.*, 1987).

This was a time of economic decline, of identity crisis for the city and its communities, of unemployment and strikes, of energy shortages and the 1970s 'Three-day Week', of the 1980s and Margaret Thatcher, the North-South divide, and political crisis and unrest (Lawless & Brown, 1986; Roberts & Sykes, 2000; Pollard & Holmes, 1976) . Miners took to the streets in protest and were brutally suppressed by police brought in from London. Coalmines closed, factories closed, land lay derelict and entire communities were out of work. Where large factories remained, they were increasingly vulnerable to being taken over by capitalists from elsewhere, outside the city or even outside the UK (Benyon *et al.*, 2000). When this happens, local people lose what control they might have had in determining their own destinies.

There were also major regional issues of competition for investment and for jobs and status with competition between Sheffield with, Leeds to the north, Nottingham to the south, and Manchester to the west. This remains a deeply divisive issue for people and for politicians.

An environmental recovery

In the 1950s, fuelled in part by a realisation and indeed the embarrassment of mass deaths due to air pollution - smog from industrial and domestic coal burning, Sheffield pioneered the idea of Clean Air and Smokeless Zones. Combined with laws to protect watercourses from pollution and to control land degradation too, this began a slow process of urban ecological renewal. Ironically, the changes were speeded by the closure of many of the factories that had been responsible for the problems. However, Sheffield once famed as the 'Dirty City in a Golden Frame' began to grow a sense of civic pride as 'The Clean Air City', and by the 1980s, as a 'Green City' (Bownes *et al.*, 1991).

From these beginnings in the 1980s, there developed an interest in the potential for a genuine renewal of the landscape and ecology of the Lower Don Valley, the city's former industrial heartland. Indeed, with little prospect on economic renewal the derelict and despoiled landscape was seen as a barrier to investment. Furthermore, even without intervention, nature was quickly reclaiming miles of unused former factory sites.

In planning and political terms, the idea of greening the valley as a precursor or even a trigger and catalyst for economic renewal gained support. Grants were available to remove pollution and to regenerate the landscape with massed tree and shrub planting, and the creation of new public open spaces and wildlife reserves. Access began of opening up riversides and canals for people to walk along and to provide much-improved footpaths and other facilities. Much of this work was led by local people determined to take action to improve their future. A planning and landscape vision for the Lower Don Valley was developed by the City Council and then by the short-lived Sheffield Development Corporation (SDC). A fast-track planning process and available finance both administered by the SDC provided catalysts for investment, renewal and re-development, and Sheffield began to turn a critical corner in its emergence as a modern city. Transformation from industrial to post-industrial was now well underway.

Figure 13: Wild figs along the urban rivers – part of a new, recombinant ecology

Emergence of a new economy

Central to the emergence of Sheffield as a modern and truly European city were a number of concepts and ideas that challenged the very roots of the industrial city's identity. The first of these was the intention to 'green' the former industrial areas and so to change perceptions about them and their possible futures (Watts *et al.*, 1987; Bownes *et al.*, 1991). The second idea, which was even more controversial, was to build Europe's largest shopping centre at Meadowhall, on former industrial land (Williams, 1991; Lawless, 1990; Roberts & Sykes, 2000). This was central to the then new concept of 'leisure shopping'. The idea was to merge retail and leisure, with food and entertainment. The third component was to brand Sheffield as the UK Sports City and to trigger this by hosting the relatively unknown 'World Student Games' in 1991. This resulted in a massive commitment to capital investment in infrastructure, a transformation of greenspace, a total renewal of transport provision to link the city centre to peripheral regions, and to thread together the sporting, leisure and retail facilities by new arterial roads and buses, by cycleway and walkways, and by a new high-tech electric Supertram. Sheffield was to become a city of sport, of shopping and leisure, and of tourism (Bramwell, 1997 a, b, 1998). For many local people this seemed more than a little far-fetched.

These steps were hugely controversial and received little political support from the national government at Westminster. This meant that a consequence for Sheffield was that in order to proceed, the City Council plunged itself and its community into a long-term debt that only now is close to being repaid. The step was a big gamble since it depended utterly on the corporate success of all these actions and interventions. The political fallout was considerable and there were casualties in the City Council. Twenty-five years on, the gamble has paid off and the vision has become a reality; even more remarkable when the lack of central government support is considered. However, on the back of regional economic planning, and forceful negotiating the region did gain two major external funding streams, both from Europe. One was the Coalfields Development Fund, for former coal mining areas, and the other Objective One status for South Yorkshire. These two financial mechanisms enabled many of the necessary infrastructure transformations to happen, without which the other economic renewals would not have taken place.

Emerging in the post-industrial era there have been a number of key economic forces:

- **Retail & Leisure**
- **Leisure & Entertainment**
- **Sport & Events**
- **Tourism – including industrial museums (the first in the world) and the Peak National Park (the first in Britain)**
- **High tech and service industries**
- **Education - with two major universities and 50,000 students**
- **Health provision and hospitals**
- **Local authority and local service provision**

The final stages – a city transformed and a region re-born

A major controversy and a problem for regional regeneration, was the tension between the Lower Don Valley and the old city centre (Williams, 1991; Roberts & Sykes, 2000). This was especially the case for the established city centre shops, which, failing to compete with the allure of Meadowhall went into a steep decline. This was always going to be the case and there were other deeply ingrained problems with city centre layout and facilities, even without the new competition. However, in the 1990s, a concept emerged called the 'Heart of the City Project' grew to provide a vision and plan for renewal of the urban centre. Again this has included new faculties, carefully deigned public spaces and greenery, spectacular artwork and a reorganised and improved transport system. Again, this has been hugely successful and its final stages are now in process. The city centre is now a transformed and vibrant area with plazas and piazzas, fountains and avenues, street cafés, museums, theatres and galleries. The modern city has a genuinely European feel about it and is popular with locals and visitors alike. With leisure day visitors and tourists, and especially international visitors because of the two universities, Sheffield is truly a city transformed.

The severe negative impacts of Meadowhall on other regional shopping and social loci such as Rotherham town centre have yet to be successfully resolved, but the city centre has responded and change is afoot.

Planning issues

The case study demonstrates a number of key innovations that challenge current thinking and twenty-first century politics. The first matter to consider (1) is the critical importance in this dramatic transformation is the role of what I define elsewhere as 'Positive Planning Interventions' (PPIs) (see Rotherham, 2015) to remove pollution and dereliction, to transform transportation infrastructures, to renew the environmental and landscape resource, and to trigger economic growth. This was initiated by Sheffield City Council in the 1980s, but then carried forwards with political and economic support from the national Conservative Government of the day, by the Sheffield Development Corporation (specifically targeting the Lower Don Valley to implement Sheffield City Council ideas, mostly with officers from the same but with enhanced finance, planning powers and essentially removed from local democratic controls). The ideas were generated by partnerships between politicians, planners, researchers from both Sheffield Universities, the business community and local people. This melting pot for innovation happed in a way that probably would not be possible today.

However, another issue (2) is significant, in that the economic transformation was led by a desire initially to 'green' the valley and to change perceptions of it as a place to live, to work, to play, and above all, to invest. The radical approach to environmental recovery in essence kick-started the subsequent transformations. The two linear features, the River Don and the Tinsley Canal, formed the spinal units of a new and robust landscape. Strategic creation of green corridors, of new walkways, and green links and nodes, were combined with massive land reclamation projects to remove centuries-old pollution. At the city centre end of the valley was the Canal Basin restoration, and at the eastern toe of the valley, was the Blackburn Meadows Urban Nature Reserve. Other core locations included the short-lived Sheffield Airport site (Cartwright et al., 2000; Anon., 1990; Watts, 1991)

The third key lesson from this research (3) is the importance of the PPIs noted above (1), in applied as interventions four main areas:

a) **Landscape and environmental quality**
b) **Economic regeneration through leisure retail**
c) **Economic regeneration through sports and leisure events**
d) **Transformation of transport infrastructure and networks**

Implementation of these interventions was ultimately made possible by the imposition from national government of a short-term 'Development Corporation'. The long-term custodianship reverted back to the Sheffield City Council. Ideas such as the 1991 World Student Games (Anon., 1988) and the creation of associated venues and other critical infrastructure were initiated and funded by Sheffield City Council with little national governmental support. However, sports and leisure events have now emerged as major catalysts for urban economic renewal (Gratton, 2004; Gratton *et al.*, 2005; Beard *et al.*, 2000). The possibilities of leisure retail and the major economic hub of Meadowhall Shopping; entre were excellent examples of public-private partnership which helped trigger wider economic renewal. Meadowhall has however had massive detrimental impact on some other local centres such as Rotherham town centre. The short-term impact on Sheffield city centre was acute and negative. Nevertheless, I argue that the impacts of the Lower Don Valley transformation and the development of Meadowhall in particular, ultimately brought about a radical change in the city centre which has been for the ultimate good.

Finally, the other major change in the city's economic landscape has been the emergence of the two universities and their combined 50,000 students and staff. This has underpinned regional tourism and associated business growth, been essential for the viability of the city centre renewal, and promoted the city on a worldwide stage. However, the link to, and dependence on, good quality environments in the city, along the River Don, and in the hinterland such as the Peak National Park, should not be under-estimated.

The changes over time in the Lower Don Valley can be related to three broad pillars of sustainable development:

- **Social Triggers**
- **Environmental Triggers**
- **Economic Catalysts**

It is these three interlinked aspects of regeneration, which combined with opportunities, and led by individual project champions, have transformed the valley, and ultimately the wider city.

Conclusions - The Triple Bottom Line

This is an interesting case study, which can help inform understanding and good practice elsewhere. However, it is important to be able to find ways to link and to interrogate the different factors that have driven the changes. Furthermore, we need to be able to assess critically and to evaluate how these changes have affected local people. In the past, economic planning and environmental issues for example, were often considered separate disciplines and the forces at play to be in opposition. In its industrial heyday, the fact that Sheffield was dirty and polluted was a source of civic pride. Dirt equalled industry equalled wealth. Yet by the 1990s, it was clear that dirt and dereliction blocked inward investment and deterred both business and tourists alike.

To meet this need there has emerged a new concept of the *'Triple Bottom Line'* of economy, environment, and community (Ma *et al.*, 2006, 2011). Evaluated and assessed together, these give a more holistic and informative insight into the forces at work in regional planning and renewal, in social, environmental and economic regeneration. Failure to recognise the interrelationships between these three components of 'sustainable development' will mean firstly lack of understanding of the processes of transformation. Secondly, it will mean that in real projects, in towns and cities around the world, opportunities will be missed and people will suffer unnecessarily.

Figure 14: Wildflower meadows along the urban River Don

There is a cost in triggering the benefits

In order to generate and to trigger recovery from downturn and dereliction we need to invest in people, in infrastructure, and in the environment. In times of economic austerity, this is not a message that today's politicians wish to hear (See Rotherham, 2014, 2015).

- Need to invest public money to draw down wider benefits of the *Triple Bottom Line* - economic, environmental, & social

- Need to recognise and celebrate the past but in a way that provides a platform and a positive vision for the future

- Need to place the community and the environment at the centre of regeneration and of the economy

- Need to foster local and regional distinctiveness to resonate with and engage the community

- Need to empower local people to take responsibility for their futures

The critical roles of PPIs in reflecting local ideas and demand, and in intervening to bring about change, are recognised as being at the core of the regeneration process (Rotherham, 2013a, b, 2015). However, also of huge importance is the inter-linking of the various processes with environmental improvement and community empowerment essential in catalysing other changes. At all levels, community champions, business leaders, university researchers and local government officers and members worked together bring about these far-reaching changes. In the face for example, of slimmed-down local authority planning services, and audit-driven university research provision, it is unlikely that such innovations and collaborations would happen today (Rotherham, 2013a, b).

In Sheffield and the Lower Don Valley, the economy and the community have been transformed, and the ecology too (Rotherham & Cartwright, 2000; Rotherham & Boon, 1988; Rotherham *et al.*, 1986). Where the River Don in the 1970s was a dead sewer of detergent foam, of raw sewage, of industrial chemical and gross thermal pollution, locked away from public access and gaze, today it too is transformed (Wild & Gilbert, 1988; Bownes et al., 1991; Rotherham, 1988). We have a clean river with twelve or more species of fish, extensive public walkways, of active recreational use, of riverside residential apartments, of new business offices, and a vibrant recombinant ecology of native and exotic species (Rotherham, 2017). Otters live and play under the dense stands of alien Japanese knotweed, and grey herons and kingfishers entertain the residents in riverside apartments in once derelict factories. This is a dramatic transformation but it required innovation, risk, and public expenditure in order to bring it about.

Figure 15: Recombinant ecology with giant hogweed on the urban rivers

Latterly, there was also recognition of the potential and actual importance of contaminated and post-industrial sites for nature conservation (e.g. Middleton, 2000; Rotherham, 1999, 2012; Rotherham *et al.*, 2005; Rotherham *et al.*, 2012). This said, beyond exciting headline sites such as Blackburn Meadows (Rotherham & Cartwright, 2001) or Old Moor in the Dearne Valley (Rotherham & Cartwright, 2001; Rotherham, 2013d) relatively little is done to capitalise on the opportunities presented by such sites (Rotherham *et al.*, 2003). It can be argued that the regeneration of the industrial lands such as the Lower Don Valley in Sheffield, and the Lower Dearne Valley in Barnsley, for example, has been significantly influence and even sometimes led by improvement in the natural environment.

Today, along the River Don in Sheffield centre, new landscaping reflects and enhances the natural recovery processes. Furthermore, the remaining historic buildings and structures like the medieval and industrial bridges and weirs, provide a heritage context and setting for the new urban renaissance. For the first time in perhaps five hundred years, people can walk through native wildflowers (and alien or recombinant ecologies too), and watch otters, herons, cormorants and kingfishers. This is a remarkable transformation.

Figure 16: River Don kingfisher photographed by Brent Hardy

References & Bibliography

Anon. (1988) Sport Aid (World Student Games to be staged in Sheffield). *The Economist* (US), September 17, 1988.

Anon. (1990) *Sheffield and Rotherham City Airport – Environmental Statement*. Shepheard Epstein and Hunter, London.

Beard, C., Egan, D. & Rotherham, I.D. (2000) *The changing role of outdoor leisure: a critical review of countryside tourism*, In: *Reflections on International Tourism. Environmental Management and Pathways to Sustainable Tourism.* Robinson, M., Swarbrooke, J., Evans, N., Long, P. and Shapley, R. (Eds.), Centre for Travel and Tourism, University of Northumbria, Sunderland, pp. 1-19.

Beynon, H., Cox, A. & Hudson, R. (2000) *Digging Up Trouble - The Environment, Protest and Opencast Coal Mining*. Rivers Oram Press, London.

Bownes, J.S., Riley, T.H., Rotherham, I.D. & Vincent, S.M. (1991) *Sheffield Nature Conservation Strategy*. Sheffield City Council, Sheffield.

Bramwell, B. (1997a) A sport mega-event as a sustainable tourism development strategy. *Tourism Recreation Research,* **22**(2), 13-19.

Bramwell, B. (1997b) Strategic Planning before and after a mega-event. *Tourism Management,* **18**(3), 167-176.

Bramwell, B. (1998) *Event tourism in Sheffield: A sustainable approach to urban development?* In: Bramwell, B., Henry, I., Jackson, G., Prat, A., Richards, G. & van der Straaten, J. (Eds.), *Sustainable tourism management: Principles & practices* Tilburg University Press, Tilburg, 147-170.

Cartwright, G., Watts, R. & Rotherham, I.D. (2000) *Airport, steelworks or historic landscapes - integrated development of Sheffield City Airport.* In: *Abstract Proceedings SER 2000*, Liverpool, Unpaged.

Gilbertson, D.D., Grattan, J.P., Cressey, M. & Pyatt, F.B. (1997) An air-pollution history of metallurgical innovation in iron- and steel-making: a geochemical archive of Sheffield. *Water, Air and Soil Pollution*, **100**, 327-341.

Goodchild, J. (ed.) (1971) The Peat-cutting Industry of South Yorkshire. *The South Yorkshire Journal*, Part Three, May 1971, 1-5.

Gratton, C. (2004) *Sport and Economic Regeneration.* Sport Industry Research Centre, Sheffield Hallam University, Sheffield.

Gratton, C., Shibli, S. & Coleman, R. (2005) Sport and economic regeneration in cities. *Urban Studies*, **42**(5/6), 1-15.

Hopkins, L.D. (2001) *Urban Development; the Logic of Making Plans.* Island Press, Washington D.C.

Hunter, J. (1819) *The History and Topography of the Parish of Sheffield: with Historical and Descriptive Notices of the Parishes of Ecclesfield, Hansworth, Treeton and*

Whiston, and of the Chapelry of Bradfield. (1869 edition) Pawson and Brailsford, Sheffield.

Lawless, P. (1990) *Regeneration in Sheffield: From Radical Intervention to Partnership.* In: Judd, D. & Parkinson, M. (Eds.) *Leadership and Urban Regeneration.* Urban Affairs Annual reviews, Volume 37, Sage Publications, London, 133-150.

Lawless, P. & Brown, F. (1986) *Urban growth and change in Britain: an introduction.* Paul Chapman Publishing Ltd., London.

Ma, S.C., Rotherham, I.D., Egan, D.J. & Ma, S.M. (2006). Sports mega-events: An approach to sustainable urban development? *City Development*, **2**, 97-126.

Ma, S.C., Rotherham, I.D., Egan, D.J. & Ma, S.M. (2011) A framework for monitoring during the planning stage for a sports mega-event. *Journal of Sustainable Tourism*, **19**, 1-18.

Middleton, P. (2000) The wildlife significance of a former colliery site in Yorkshire. *British Wildlife*, **11**, 333-339.

Pollard, S. & Holmes, C. (1976) *Essays in the Economic and Social History of South Yorkshire.* South Yorkshire County Council, Barnsley.

Rackham, O. (1986) *The History of the Countryside.* J.M. Dent & Sons Ltd, London.

Roberts, P. & Sykes, H. (2000) *Urban Regeneration: A Handbook.* SAGE Publications, London.

Rotherham, I.D. (1988) *Tinsley Park – Further comments on the land within the B.S.C. Complex*. Sheffield City Ecology Unit, Sheffield.

Rotherham, I.D. (2012) Post Coal-mining Landscapes: water, heaths, and commons as a resource for wildlife, people and heritage. In: Rotherham, I.D. & Handley, C. (eds) (2012) Between a Rock and A Hard Place. *Landscape Archaeology and Ecology Special Series*. Papers from the Landscape Conservation Forum, (2), Wildtrack Publishing, Sheffield, 49-58.

Rotherham, I.D. (2013a) *The impacts on active countryside tourism of the rise and fall of countryside management*. Proceedings of Active Countryside Tourism, Leeds, 23-25 January 2013, Leeds, 18 pages.

Rotherham, I.D. (2013b) *The economic implications of countryside recreation and sports: a review*. Proceedings of Active Countryside Tourism, Leeds, 23-25 January 2013, Leeds, 11 pages.

Rotherham, I.D. (2013c) *Lost Sheffield in Colour*. Amberley Publishing, Stroud.

Rotherham, I.D (2013d) New entrepreneurs in conservation - how the RSPB kick-started tourism in South Yorkshire's Dearne Valley. *ECOS*, **34**, 5-11.

Rotherham, I.D. (2014) *Eco-History: A Short History of Conservation and Biodiversity*. The White Horse Press, Cambridge.

Rotherham, I.D. (2015) *Lost Sheffield in Colour*. Amberley Publishing, Stroud.

Rotherham, I.D. (2017) *Recombinant Ecology – a hybrid future?* Springer Briefs, Springer, Dordrecht. (in press).

Rotherham, I.D. & Boon, G. (1988) *A Preliminary Assessment of the Ecological Value of Tinsley Park (SK 405 884); and Geology of Tinsley Park Area. Natural Sciences Section.* City Museum, Sheffield.

Rotherham, I.D. & Cartwright G. (2000) The potential of Urban Wetland Conservation in economic and environmental renewal - a case study approach. *Practical Ecology and Conservation*, **4(1)**, 47-60.

Rotherham, I.D. & Cartwright G. (2001) *Urban Wetland Conservation - case studies in environmental and economic renewal.* In: Atherden, M. (Ed.) *Wetlands in the Landscape: archaeology, conservation, heritage.* PLACE Research Centre, York. pp. 150-154.

Rotherham, I.D., Cartwright, G. & Boon, G. (1986) *Lower Don Valley Wildlife and Geology: A preliminary report.* Natural Sciences Section, City Museum, Sheffield.

Rotherham, I.D., Doncaster, S. & Egan, D. (2005) Nature-based Leisure and Tourism in England's Humberhead Levels. *Annals of Tourism Research*, **8**(2-3), 214-230.

Rotherham, I.D., Spode, F. & Fraser, D. (2003) *Post–coalmining landscapes: an under-appreciated resource for wildlife, people and heritage.* In: Moore, H.M., Fox, H.R. & Elliot, S. (Eds.) *Land Reclamation: extending the boundaries.* Published: A.A. Balkema Publishers, Lisse. 93-99.

Tacoli, C. (ed.) *The Earthscan Reader in Rural-Urban Linkages*. Earthscan, London.

Smout, C. (2001) *Nature Contested*. Edinburgh University Press, Edinburgh.

Walton, M. (1948) *Sheffield: Its Story and its Achievements*. The Sheffield Telegraph & Star Limited, Sheffield.

Watts, R. (1991) *Tinsley Park Opencast Landscape Brief*. Department of Land and Planning, Sheffield City Council, Sheffield.

Watts, R., Pearson, R. & Rotherham, I.D. (1987) *New Life for the Lower Don Valley. Landscape Design*, **165**, 16-19.

Wild, M. & Gilbert, O.L. (1988) *Sheffield Inner City Habitat Survey*. Sheffield City Wildlife Group, Sheffield.

Williams, J.L. (1991) Meadowhall: Its Impact on Sheffield City Centre and Rotherham. *International Journal of Retail & Distribution Management*, **19** (1), 29-37.

Williamson, J.G. (1990) *Coping with city growth during the British industrial revolution*. Cambridge University Press, Cambridge.

Regulating a Pre-Modern, Industrial, Urban Landscape: Street Cleaning, Waste-disposal and Insanitary Nuisances in Sheffield, 1500-1700

Dr Leona Skelton,
University of Bristol

In the sixteenth and seventeenth centuries, urban governors faced sanitation problems of a markedly different character than those faced by town and city councils today. Malodours emanating from soap-boiling, slaughterhouses, candle-making, tanners' and dyers' vats, open drainage channels, dunghills, stables and pig sties characterized pre-modern, urban streets. Not a few contemporaries were engaged in a combination of domestic, industrial and agricultural activities in the same neighbourhoods, streets and even within the bounds of one property because craftsmen's workshops were commonly situated above, below or behind their homes, to facilitate economic familial survival. In addition, small agricultural outbuildings, such as pig sties, hen houses or stables, were common features of the areas of land behind houses and dunghills and free-roaming livestock peppered the urban landscape. Sheffield's sanitation was shaped by these general urban problems which were nationally widespread, but the town's sanitation was distinctive in several important ways. Unlike many of its English counterparts, Sheffield was not governed by an urban corporation. Its manorial governors delegated urban management to a team of Town Trustees, known as the Church Burgesses or collectively as the

Burgery, whose responsibilities included appointing two constables, a beadle and a bellman each year, arranging the maintenance of sewers, bridges and thoroughfares and administering payments to the poor. Manorial courts, known as the Great Court Leet which was held twice a year in April and October and the Court Baron which was held every three weeks, regulated Sheffield's proto-industrial landscape which featured many smithies; the waste produced in smithies was known locally as 'smithie sleck'. In comparison to sanitation and insanitary nuisances in many other British towns during this period, the references to industry and industrial nuisances in the urban landscape in Sheffield's court minutes and constables' accounts are particularly striking, especially in the context of its relatively modest size and demography.[1] Using a range of sources, including court records, constables' accounts, church burgesses' accounts, travel literature and property surveys, this paper will reveal much about Sheffield's developing industrial landscape in the sixteenth and seventeenth centuries through the very useful lens of sanitation and the regulation of insanitary nuisances. Looking at the early history of Sheffield's industrial landscape through the lens of sanitation provides very deep insights because the documentary records which relate to sanitation provide a direct route to the heart of daily life as it was experienced at all social levels in the town.

Significant volumes of waste were produced in the town, of which domestic waste constituted only a relatively small proportion compared to agricultural and industrial waste. Manure could be used to fertilise one's own arable holdings

---

[1] Population estimates suggest that Sheffield's population rose from around 2,200 in 1600 to 3,500 by 1700. See S. Pollard, 'The Growth of Population', in D. L. Linton, (ed.), *Sheffield and its Region: A Scientific and Historical Survey* (Sheffield, 1956), p. 172.

or sold to local rural farmers, but it was often built up into a substantial heap, known as a midding or a dunghill, before it was sold or removed from inhabitants' property frontages or backlands. Domestic and industrial waste included: dirty water from cooking, cleaning and washing; food waste and bones; hearth ashes; building waste, such as rubble and broken stones; and small amounts of non-organic material such as glass and metal. Most contemporaries recycled food waste, by feeding it to livestock, and they sold unwanted possessions, especially clothes, out of necessity, which limited how much waste was produced.[2] Rubbish, often termed 'rubbidge', and manure was usually hauled using pack horses or in horse-drawn carts or sledges to the surrounding countryside where rubbish could be buried and manure could be sold to farmers to be used as fertilizer. Where there was sufficient space, rubbish pits could be dug on one's own land, obviating the transportation of rubbish out of town. When some building work was undertaken on Sheffield Parish Church, in 1622, the Church Burgesses paid a labourer 7d for 'making a pitt & removing of plankes & Rubbish'; whereas in 1691, they chose instead to pay 1s 2d 'for carriage of Rubbish'.[3] Perhaps, by this point, the Church Burgesses had run out of open space in which to dig rubbish pits. In 1578, at Sheffield Great Court Leet, it was recorded that Lawrence Shemeld, the wife of Sawood, Thomas Harison & Robert Stanyfurth, a painter, had laid 'certeine Mainor [i.e. manure] or dounge in the hie stretes contrarie to a paine laid' for which they were each fined 4d.[4] That four people were fined in unison suggests that

---

[2] B. Lemire, 'Consumerism in pre-industrial and early industrial England: the trade in second-hand clothes', *Journal of British Studies*, 27 (1988), pp. 1-24.
[3] Sheffield Archives, [hereafter SA], CB/161: Sheffield Church Burgesses' Account Book, 1574-1727.
[4] SA, ACM/S/116: A Book of Pains and Amerciaments, Sheffield Court Leet, 1578 (03/04/1578).

they contributed their respective waste to a common dunghill which they accumulated in one location. Although neighbourhood dunghills could be quite large-scale features used by a large number of households, they could also be much smaller products of only a few people's waste.

Sheffield was situated on a prominent ridge, and benefited from the very steep and favourable gradients down to the natural receptacle of the River Don for its drainage. However, the drainage of rainwater and liquid waste away from businesses and dwellings still presented complex challenges to the town's governors. In April 1609, Sheffield's Court Leet Jurors made a record which confirms that they made householders responsible for maintaining some, if not all, of the town's drainage infrastructure. They recorded 'a paine that Thomas Horner shall scour his ditch after Sisottfield side and keepe the water in the right course that it breake not into the laine at Upperthorpe gate before Penticost next and so to keep the same at all times' under the pain of 10s.[5] Although householders were still largely responsible for maintaining a sanitary standard around their homes, and sanitation was far more hands on and beholden to the compliance and efforts of householders than it is today, some elements of the town's drainage infrastructure were maintained by Sheffield Burgery, as the constables' accounts demonstrate. In 1614, for example, the constables were paying a Beadle to undertake a large range of outdoor maintenance tasks around the town. In 1614, Steven the Beadle received a weekly wage of 16d and a new livery coat each year made from cloth buttons and silk which cost between 9s and 11s 4d.[6] From at least 1649, the Beadle was

---

[5] *Records of the Burgery of Sheffield, commonly called the Town Trust*, ed. J. Leader (London: Elliot Stock, 1897), p. 315.
[6] SA, Jackson Collection 905: Sheffield Constables' Accounts, 1615-1677.

named as George Bower every year until at least 1657 and a Bellman and a swineherd were employed in a similar way.[7] In addition to these long-term positions, the Burgery also made *ad hoc* payments on a casual basis for extra duties. In 1682, for example, Sheffield Burgery paid 6d for 'mending the Truelove gutter with Lime and sand'; but by 1688, it had been 'then agreed by the Trustees present that John Webster shall have allowed him 30s for money laid out for scoureing and repering the Truelove gutter'.[8] In 1568, they paid 12d to Nicholas Grynne for 'kepinge the church walles cleane' and in 1623 they paid 4s 'for sweeping the Bridge and pavement att the churchgates'.[9]

Towards the end of the seventeenth century, we can see administrative changes which point to real progress in terms of the centralisation and better organisation of sanitation services. A Scavenger was paid 1 li per year from 1683 to at least 1700 whereas before 1683, particular labourers were paid for tasks such as cleansing the night soil buckets or for repairing the house of office [i.e. toilet], at the Almshouse.[10] *Ad hoc* tasks continued alongside this more regular system, however, as in 1691, the burgesses listed a payment of 3s 6d to Robert Spencer for 'leading the rubbish from Mr Leech house'.[11] Householders in Sheffield would have had a good level of understanding about where the line lay between theirs and their urban governors' sanitation obligations as bylaws and waste disposal arrangements were read aloud in public places and

---

[7] SA, Jackson Collection 905: Sheffield Constables' Accounts, 1615-1677.
[8] *Records of the Burgery of Sheffield*, pp. 219, 242.
[9] SA, CB/159: Church Burgesses' Account Book, 1557-1574; *Records of the Burgery of Sheffield*, p. 220.
[10] *Records of the Burgery of Sheffield*, p. 259.
[11] SA, CB/161: Church Burgesses' Account Book, 1574-1727.

contraventions of bylaws were presented and fined at public court hearings.

While Sheffield Burgery did not employ any specific street-cleaners or even an official scavenger until 1683, it did maintain an ingenious mechanism to aid inhabitants' street cleaning. In 1572, a small, man-made reservoir, called Barker's Pool, situated at the highest point in the west of the town, near the market place, was walled and fitted with sluice gates which opened into each of the main, salient streets descending from it. During dry weather, when sweeping the streets became difficult and dirt started to accumulate, these sluice gates were opened and water flowed down the streets to enable householders to sweep their forefronts. The water descended Fargate, High Street, Market Street, Water Lane and then down into the River Don.[12] Barker's Pool was cleaned out, kept watertight and repaired at the Burgery's expense throughout the period. In 1572, for example, 6d was paid 'to Thomas Creswyke for a shotle [i.e. shuttle or sluice gate] to Barkers Powle'.[13] And, in 1636, 1s 6d was paid 'to James Hodgson for feying [i.e. cleaning] and keeping of Barkers Poole'.[14] This unique mechanism is an insightful example of town authorities' endeavours to keep the urban landscape clean in this period. Perhaps it was Barker's Pool which caused The Earl of Oxford's Chaplain to comment in 1725 on 'the health of the place, which few towns so populous enjoy with such constancy as they do'; he specifically mentioned Barker's pool, noting the inhabitants' 'opportunity of sweeping into it all their uncleanly encumbrances'.[15]

---

[12] D. Hey, *A History of Sheffield* (Lancaster: Carnegie, 1998), p. 57.
[13] *Records of the Burgery of Sheffield*, p. 27.
[14] *Records of the Burgery of Sheffield*, p. 136.
[15] Hey, *History of Sheffield*, p. 57.

Dirty water from food preparation and cooking, washing dishes, domestic cleaning and washing clothes could threaten the purity of drinking water supplies. Although most women disposed of dirty water carefully into drainage channels or large rivers, some townswomen washed clothes and cleaned other items in or near to wells, which was expressly forbidden. At Sheffield's Great Court Leet, in April 1609, inhabitants were warned under the threat of a fine of 3s 4d,

> 'That no person or persons shall at any time hereafter wash any clothes, calfe heads, calfe meates or ... other things within three yarde of the Towne Head Well, New Hall Well, Burtland Well or any other common well in and about the same towne for corruptinge the said wells.'[16]

In most towns, householders were expected to keep clear, to sweep clean and to pave the area before their property to the middle of the street (the forefront) once weekly, usually on Saturday nights after the weekly market and before the Sabbath. Forefronts on main streets were legally part of the King's highway, and therefore Crown property, but householders were made responsible for their own sections by the means of local bylaws. In 1578, Sheffield's Court Leet Jurors threatened 'a paine that everye persoune inhabitinge within the Towne of Sheffeld shall have the strete againste his dore where it hath bene accustomed to be paved before Michelmasse next' under the pain of 6s 8d.[17] Keeping the streets passable and the thoroughfares flowing was vital to efficient trade, and although the Burgery funded some of the work in this respect, householders were still ultimately responsible for the street and the open sewer passing in front of their property, known as their forefront.

---

[16] *Records of the Burgery of Sheffield*, p. 312.
[17] SA, ACM/S/116: A Book of Pains and Amerciaments, 1578 (03/04/1578).

In 1609, at the Great Court Leet, an order was issued to the householders of several streets,

> 'All and every person and persons which have any grounds adjoininge or buttinge on Sheremore, Sheremore laine, Mortoune wheele laine, Upperthorpe laine, Brockway hill laine, Gillcarr laine, blind laine, Cole pitt laine, or any of them, doe skower and clense their ditches and water courses ther as hertofore have been pained and accustomed. And doe cutt the banks of the ditches ther so that the water may have passage and be continually kept in the right courses and snath and brush ther hedges and fences ther that carriages may pass without any interruption before Penticost next and so to keepe the same at all times, in paine of every one not doing his or ther duties therin to forfeite for every defaulte [to be fined 3s 4d]'[18]

In this extract, we can see that maintaining the flow of horse-drawn traffic and trade was as, if not more, important than maintaining the cleanliness of the urban environment. The manorial courts also regulated building encroachments, such as in 1578 when Thomas Webster enclosed 'a felde and a garden of the waste & hath builded halfe a smethie of the same in the tenure of Nicholas Perkin'.[19] Smithies were common features in early modern Sheffield. For example, in 1671, the Burgesses leased to Elizabeth Wood, of Sheffield 'all that cottage or dwelling house with the Outshutt & Smithies thereto belonging scituate & beinge in Sheffield aforesd in a certain street there called the

---

[18] Great Court Leet Roll, (18/04/1609), in *Records of the Burgery of Sheffield*, p. 312.
[19] SA, ACM/S/116: A Book of Pains and Amerciaments, 1578, (03/04/1578).

Westbarr'.[20] This property clearly had more than one smithy, but it does not state exactly how many. In 1609, in a typical order issued to all of the inhabitants of one street called Church Lane, a particular waste product known locally as 'smethie sleck' is listed among the other types of rubbish to be removed as a matter of course.

> 'A payne laid that all those howsholders dweling in the Church layne between Widow Jacksons house and George Fox his house before Penticost next shall remoove and carry all such myre, smythie sleck, and filth, being in the towne streate against ther houses every one so far as ther howse reacheth And from [this] tyme forth keepe the same stret clensed every one against ther own howse And not to cast any sweepeinges of ther howses, smythies sleck or other things which shall hinder the water passage in payne of every of them to forfeit.'[21]

Smithy sleck is mentioned here as if it were as common as any other type of domestic waste.

In 1637, John Harrison, a Norfolk Surveyor was commissioned by the Howards to conduct a detailed survey of Sheffield, and he described,

> 'The River of Donn drownes the name of the other River called the Sheath. Besides those two Rivers there are other Rivers called porter water Loxley water & Rwclin water, w[hi]ch other small Rivers & brookes. These Rivers are very proffitable unto the Lord in regard of the Mills and Cutterwheeles that are

---

[20] SA, MD 1037-1050: Deeds Relating to Sheffield Market Place, 1610-1722: MD 1044: Indenture between Church Burgesses of Sheffield and Elizabeth Wood, (20/03/1671).
[21] Great Court Leet Roll, 18/04/1609, in *Records of the Burgery of Sheffield*, p. 312.

turned by their streames wch wheeles are imployed for the grindinge of knives by foure or five hundred Maister workemen that gives severall marks.'[22]

In this productive and increasingly industrial urban landscape, smithies were built in and among residential dwellings and agricultural barns, orchards, communal dung heaps and industrial edifices such as tanning pits, slaughterhouses and skinning workhouses. In 1637, John Harrison noted that Kenelme Holmer 'holdeth at will a Cottage w[i]th a Stable a Smithey, a Garden & a Backside lyinge in Sheffeild towne and abbutt upon a way next the Tan house and payeth yearly' 4d.[23] He also noted that Anne Clayton 'holdeth at will a Cowhouse and a Garden and payeth no rent for it' and that Lawrence Bradbury 'holdeth a Cottage w[i]th a Smithey in High street neere Margrett Greenwood South east: Also a Midden stead' and he paid a yearly rent of 5s 6d.[24] Demonstrating the diverse range of agricultural, domestic and industrial activities undertaken on one plot, Harrison also listed 'a tenement with a dwelling house, a mault house, a barne, a stable, an orchard [and] a garden lying in sheffield towne next a way east and coulson croft west certain gardens north and west barr south'.[25] While through modern-day eyes, early modern Sheffield might have looked like a very large village, retaining many aspects of its unspecialised medieval household economy, we could not fail to notice the very well developed industrial activity being conducted in and

---

[22] SA, ACM/S/75: John Harrison, 'An Exact and Perfect Survey of the Manor of Sheffield', 1637.
[23] SA, ACM/S/75: John Harrison, 'An Exact and Perfect Survey of the Manor of Sheffield', 1637.
[24] SA, ACM/S/75: John Harrison, 'An Exact and Perfect Survey of the Manor of Sheffield', 1637.
[25] SA, ACM/S/75: John Harrison, 'An Exact and Perfect Survey of the Manor of Sheffield', 1637.

around the urban agriculture, together with the trading and the activities of daily urban life.

Free-roaming livestock was a common nuisance on the streets of early modern Sheffield, although there was a pinfold near Barker's Pool which was maintained at the expense of the Burgery. In 1597, for example, 2s 10d was paid for 'wood and bordes for the pinfold dore and staples, pick and making the same'.[26] Allowing livestock to roam freely was such a serious offence because free-roaming swine or geese could deposit their own waste on the streets, and swine could eat and trample crops, rummage in sewers or even in graves and charge into market stalls and dunghills, damaging goods and spreading carefully piled animal manure across the streets. In 1578, Robert Bower was fined 12d at the Lord's Court 'for that he kept not his swine ringd viz three swine'.[27] Nicholas Bomforth was also fined 2s 4d for keeping seven swine unringed.[28]

Dunghills were common features on sixteenth- and seventeenth-century Sheffield's streets, but they were only regulated when they had been left unremoved for too long, when they physically blocked thoroughfares, when they were unbearably malodorous or when they encroached into neighbouring properties. They were valuable, useful and ubiquitous features of the urban landscape rather than as totally useless and annoying waste products to be expelled from town as soon as possible. Some townsmen paid formal rents in order to build dunghills on someone else's land. For example, in 1566, William Sklatter paid 4d per year for a

---

[26] *Records of the Burgery of Sheffield*, p. 191.
[27] SA, ACM/S/116: A Book of Pains and Amerciaments, 1578, (03/04/1578).
[28] SA, ACM/S/116: A Book of Pains and Amerciaments, 1578, (03/04/1578).

dunghill stead and Thomas Robinson paid 2d for one.[29] Sometimes, townsmen even fought over this valuable commodity, as this record entered into the Burgery's records in 1683 demonstrates,

> 'Att a meeting of the Townsmen then present ... there being a dispute about a middin stead adioyneing to Georg Brucks house whether the same did of right belong to Francis Brownell or to the said George Brucke. It appeared to the satisfaction of all the freeholders aforenamed that the tenants right of the said Middenstead did belong to George Brucke and ought to goe with the house in his occupacion whereto it adioynes.'[30]

> '[It was] then ordered by the persons abovesaid that Mr Thomas Diston shall have a Lease of the aforesaid house and middenstead (with the consent of the said George Brucke and his sonnes) for the term of 100 years under yearly rent with ordinary covenants and alsoe a Covenant that the said Mr Diston doe disburse to the wallers 4s in buildinge upon the place. The said Mr Diston promised to submitt to such rent as att next meeting shall be agreed on.'[31]

Although industrial activity was growing and developing, it is important to remain mindful of the large extent to which such activities co-existed with agricultural activity on the same streets, and sometimes even within the bounds of the same properties, in early modern Sheffield.

Just as early modern Berwick on Tweed's sanitation was heavily shaped by its salmon processing industry, and

---

[29] *Records of the Burgery of Sheffield*, p. 178.
[30] *Records of the Burgery of Sheffield*, p. 279, (18/06/1683).
[31] *Records of the Burgery of Sheffield*, p. 279, (18/06/1683).

Scarborough's was shaped by its proximity to its beaches and its extraction of useful oils from seals to be used in the leather industry and Newcastle on Tyne's sanitation was influenced by its large-scale trading port, Sheffield's was characterised by its ubiquitous smithies. Industrial activity in Sheffield flourished alongside urban agriculture, heaps of manure, markets and daily life. But all of these aspects of Sheffield life were managed and regulated successfully in ways which historians have tended to overlook. Only three decades ago, Lawrence Stone asserted that there was an 'almost total ignorance of...public hygiene' in early modern England.[32] More recently, in 2007, Emily Cockayne published a monograph presenting a highly selective, and unrepresentative, list of the worst examples of sensory experiences in early modern London, Oxford, Bath and Manchester.[33] But if we were to step onto the streets of Sheffield in the sixteenth or seventeenth centuries, while we would perceive somewhat chaotic street scenes featuring a lot more muck and malodours than we are used to today, we would also see people, businesses, industries and transportation functioning within collectively upheld parameters of what was acceptable and what was unacceptable in the minds of the people who called the town's neighbourhoods their home. Instead of imagining the contents of chamber pots cascading from upstairs windows into streets which resembled open sewers, which was far more common in the eighteenth and nineteenth centuries than it was before 1700, it would perhaps be more accurate to imagine an industrious urban population which lived and worked in a busy and bustling townscape featuring urban industry, agriculture, livestock and manure,

---

[32] L. Stone, *The Family, Sex and Marriage in England 1500-1800* (London, 1979), p. 62.
[33] E. Cockayne, *Hubbub: Filth, Noise and Stench in England, 1600-1770* (London, 2007).

but one which its people managed very carefully and successfully to maintain within standards which were acceptable to them.

References

Primary

Records of the Burgery of Sheffield, commonly called the Town Trust, ed. J. Leader (London: Elliot Stock, 1897).

Sheffield Archives, Shoreham Street, Sheffield

CB/159: Church Burgesses' Account Book, 1557-1574.
CB/161: Sheffield Church Burgesses' Account Book, 1574-1727.
ACM/S/116: A Book of Pains and Amerciaments, Sheffield Court Leet, 1578.
Jackson Collection 905: Sheffield Constables' Accounts, 1615-1677.
MD 1037-1050: Deeds Relating to Sheffield Market Place, 1610-1722.
ACM/S/75: John Harrison, 'An Exact and Perfect Survey of the Manor of Sheffield', 1637.

Secondary

Cockayne, E., *Hubbub: Filth, Noise and Stench in England, 1600-1770* (London, 2007).
Hey, D., *A History of Sheffield* (Lancaster: Carnegie, 1998).
Lemire, B., 'Consumerism in pre-industrial and early industrial England: the trade in second- hand clothes', *Journal of British Studies*, 27 (1988), pp. 1-24.

Pollard, S., 'The Growth of Population', in Linton, D. L., (ed.), *Sheffield and its Region: A Scientific and Historical Survey* (Sheffield, 1956).

Stone, L., *The Family, Sex and Marriage in England 1500-1800* (London, 1979).

The Wentworth-Fitzwilliams of Wentworth Woodhouse: Industrial Entrepreneurs for Three Centuries

Melvyn Jones

Introduction

For roughly three centuries in the archives of the successive owners of Wentworth Woodhouse, from the 2nd Earl of Strafford in the 1650s until 1947 and the nationalisation of their collieries when the 8th Earl Fitzwilliam was head of the estate, there have survived detailed records of the careful management of the resources on their vast estates, principally wood, timber, ironstone and coal. These resources were used to found and sustain a prodigious and immensely profitable industrial enterprise which had a profound impact on the landscape, settlement patterns and the social geography of the areas concerned. This paper, devoted principally to their South Yorkshire estates, will consider the growth and legacy of their woodland management, ironstone mining, coal mining and iron manufacturing enterprises.

The Family, the House and the Estate

During the three centuries covered by this study the heads of the family included one earl of Strafford, two marquises of Rockingham and five earls Fitzwilliam. In 1782 on the death of the 2nd Marquis the family estate included 18,000 acres (7,300 hectares) in South Yorkshire, 90,000 acres (36,400 hectares) in Ireland in counties Kildare and Wicklow, with additional properties in Northamptonshire

(3026 acres (1225 hectares)) and in North Yorkshire (in and around Malton). When the nephew of the second Marquis, the fourth Earl Fitzwilliam inherited the estates in 1782 he brought with him an estate of more than 20,000 acres around the family seat at Milton near Peterborough. Their main seat at Wentworth Woodhouse, between Barnsley and Rotherham, which still stands, though the aristocratic title was extinguished in 1979 with the death of the 10th Earl Fitzwilliam, is now a private residence. It is unusual in that it consists of two great houses built back to back. Facing west and not visible from the park is a house built in the florid Baroque style by the First Marquis's architect, Henry Flitcroft begun in 1724. In 1732 work began on an eastward facing mansion in the Palladian style. The East Front is about 606 feet long, the longest country house front in England (Figure 1).

Figure 1. Wentworth Woodhouse, the Palladian front.

Woodland Management

The woods on the Wentworth-Fitzwilliam estates were not principally to preserve game or to beautify the landscape, important though those functions were. Most of their woods were **industrial treescapes**. These woods, which by the mid-eighteenth century covered nearly 1450 acres (586 hectares) in South Yorkshire and 2100 acres (850 hectares) in Ireland, were intensively managed as coppices-with-standards. They therefore provided two distinct products: timber for building projects (including industrial projects), and wood for charcoal and a variety of crafts. Bark from the oak standards and oak coppice was also sold to local leather tanneries. Two examples will show the estate's attitude to their woodland resource.

The first example comes from two management plans drawn up in the 1st Marquis's own hand in 1727 and 1749 (WWM A 1273). In 1727 Thomas Wentworth, 1st Marquis of Rockingham, who inherited the Wentworth estates in 1723, devised what he called 'A Scheme for making a yearly considerable Profit of Spring Woods in Yorkshire' and in 1749 what he described as 'A Scheme for a Regular Fall of Wood for 21 years ...' (Figure 2). In the 1749 scheme, a 21-year rotation was used so that the woods coppiced in 1749 would be cut again in 1771, or as the Marquis put it '...& so begin the Circle again'. This meant that the Marquis' 876 acres (355 hectaes) of coppice-with-standards woodland in South Yorkshire at that time would produce a regular crop of 40 acres of underwood each year. The Marquis stipulated that there were to be five black barks (mature timber trees, 40-60 years old) and 70 wavers (sapling timber trees) left in every acre of felled coppice. The Marquis of Rockingham was fortunate that on his estate, besides hundreds of acres of coppice woods he also had deposits of ironstone, and he linked the charcoaling of the former with the mining of the latter. In 1749 he wrote that 'whereas it is the Iron Men that keep up the Price of the Wood, especiall care must be taken that the Iron Stone be never let for a longer time than the Woods are agreed for' (WWM A1273).

> A Scheme for a Regular Fall of Wood for 21 Years to come from the Year 1749 of about 42 Acres a Year the Coppice Woods in Yorkshire amounting to about nine Hundred Acres, in which Calculation Scholes Wood, all timber Trees & Woods in the Park at Wentworth are not included, nor the Woods in Northamptonshire, particularly Withmail Park of 100 Acres nor a Wood of about 30 Acres at Yesthrop Park which was felled Anno 1726 – Reserves to be at least 5 Black Barks & 70 Wavers – Philip Wood 2 Acres 2 Roods being Holted is not included nor the Wood by the Pyramide.

			Acres
Tinsley Park at Nine Falls for the Years 1749, 1750, 1751, 1752 1753, 1754, 1755, 1756 & 1757			350
Anno 1758	Bassingthorp Spring		37
Anno 1759	Great Thorncliffe		37
Anno 1760	Harley Spring 18^A Luke Spring 8 – 2 Goss Wood 8 Acres Bank Spring 4 Acres	totall	38 – 2
Anno 1761	Giles Wood 24 Acres King's Wood 11 Normandale Springs 5 Bolderfall 2A 2R	totall	42 – 2
Anno 1762	Tindle Brig Spring 4A 2R Wadsworth Spring 1 – 2R Westfield Ing Spring 3 Acres Simon Wood 25 – 2R Birkfield Spring 7^A – 2^R Coney Garth Spring 2^A – 2^R	totall	43 – 2
1763	Law Wood – 40 Acres		40 – 0
1764	Street Wood – 13 Rowing Spring 4^A – 2^R Littlewood Ing Spg 5 Acres 2 Roods Thorncliff Bottoms 5^A Blackmoor Bottoms 1^A Longland Spring & Longley Bottoms 5^A Little Thorncliffe 3	totall	37 – 0
1765, 1766, 1767 upper Linthwait 5^A – 2^R Golden being three Years Fall Smithys 4 Rainbergh 115		totall	124 – 2
38 acres Per Annum			
Anno 1768, 1769 & 1770 Westwood exclusive of all Wasts being a Fall of 42 Acres Per Year. & so begin the Circle again			126 – 0
excluding all wast to fall			876

> N.B. no Spinneys or Plantations in Wentworth Park & Demesnes are Included – There are also some little Reins & Spinneys up and down not taken notice of – also hedge Rows A Wood at Yesthorpe Park 30 Acres
>
> 1749
>
> have now bought 400 Acres more called Edlington Wood 1750 bought Ld Gallway's Estate in Hoyland on which is 60 acres of wood so now the woodland is encreased near one half of that which may be brought into Regular Falls

Figure 2. Woodland management plan 1749 by the First Marquis of Rockingham. *Wentworth Woodhouse Muniments in Sheffield Archives, WWM 1273*

The second example is the result of analyzing contents of the estate woodland account books for Ecclesall Woods from 1751 to 1901 (Jones & Walker, 1997). These woods covering some 300 acres came into the hands of the 2nd Marquis of Rockingham in 1752 on his marriage to Mary Bright. They remained as part of the Wentworth estate until

1927 when they were sold to Sheffield Corporation. The account books show clearly the gradual change from coppice woods to high forest. Only **falls of wood or coppice** were recorded in the account books from 1756 to 1847. Falls of wood were also recorded from 1848 to 1852 and from 1856 to 1859. After 1859 sales of falls of wood were **never** recorded again in the 42 years up to 1901. In 1848 a **timber sale** was recorded for the first time. A further timber sale took place in 1851 and then continuously from 1856 until the records end in 1901.

The annual account books also record meticulously the purchasers of wood and timber from Ecclesall Woods and these too reflect the changing structure of the woods. Richard Swallow of the charcoal-fired Chapeltown furnace who was the buyer of falls of wood in Ecclesall Woods in the second half of the 1770s continued to be the buyer of all the falls of wood in Ecclesall Woods until 1801. The main product in this period was, therefore, underwood poles for the making of charcoal. Ecclesall Woods contain several hundred charcoal hearths and a memorial to George Yardley, wood collier, who was burned to death in his cabin in 1787 (Figure 3).

From 1819 to 1834 the buyers of falls of wood were Newton Chambers who set up their first coke-fired blast furnace at Thorncliffe near Chapeltown in 1793. They rented the Thorncliffe site from Earl Fitzwilliam so it is not surprising that they turned to the Earl to supply them with pit timber for their collieries and ironstone mines and to provide sleepers for the extensive network of railways in and about their Thorncliffe Ironworks. By the mid-1830s industrial buyers had disappeared and were replaced by timber merchants. Abraham Windle or Windle & Baker, timber merchants, with premises in Sheffield, at Wortley and at Deepcar bought the falls of wood or falls of timber from 1835 until 1864. John Goodwin, timber merchant, bought a fall of timber in 1865, Joseph Smith, also a timber merchant, bought the timber in 1866 and 1867, and three buyers, John Swinscoe, Joseph Smith and William Toplis, again all timber merchants, bought the timber in 1868. Then with the exception of the years 1870 and 1881 and 1882 when George Rawlins, another timber merchant from Gleadless, was the buyer, William Toplis was the only buyer until the last surviving account book in 1901.

It is also interesting to note that the heads of the Wentworth estate 'exported' their entrepreneurial attitude to woodland management to their Irish estate (Jones, 1986). For example, in the mid-eighteenth century they owned 30 coppice-with-standards woodlands in County Wicklow covering 2100 acres (850 hectares) with 105 acres coming onto the market every year. Half of the Irish annual estate income in the eighteenth century came from the sales of wood, bark and timber.

Figure 3. Monument to the wood collier, George Yardley in Ecclesall Woods.

Ironstone Mining

Most travellers up and down the M1 between junctions 35 and 36 looking to the west onto what is now Tankersley Park golf course must wonder why there are rows of giant mole hills running across the golf course. These are in fact the spoil heaps of ironstone bell pits (Figure 4). They were shallow ironstone pits sunk to mine the Tankersley Ironstone, the Swallow Wood Ironstone (also known as White Mine) and Lidget Ironstone. The pits belonged to the Wentworth-Fitzwilliams and the ironstone mined to the north of the park and within the park was destined for Elsecar Ironworks and Milton Ironworks in Hoyland. Ironstone in the south of the parish was mined by Newton Chambers for their Thorncliffe Ironworks.

Ironstone had been mined in shallow bell pits in the southern parts of Tankersley parish before 1795 to supply the Chapel (Chapeltown) Furnace. Ironstone mining was then greatly expanded with the opening of Newton Chambers Ironworks at Thorncliffe in 1793, the Elsecar Ironworks in 1795 and Milton Ironworks between1799-1802 (Jones, 1995). Ironstone mining took place in the south of the parish beyond the boundary of the deer park by Newton Chambers, at Hood Hill for the Elsecar Ironworks until 1836, north of Tankersley Park for Milton Ironworks until 1841, at Bell Ground in the centre of the park between 1823 and 1858, from a deep engine pit in the park for Milton Ironworks between 1840 and 1850, again in the centre of the park in the 1850s and finally, again for both Milton Ironworks and Elsecar Ironworks from a deep engine pit at Skiers Spring to the east of the park from 1849 to 1879. Ironstone mining ceased in 1879.

In 1851 there were 251 ironstone miners working in the gin pits in Tankersley Park and two deep pits, one within the park and the other just to east of the park boundary at Skiers Spring. Because the mining was taking place in a former deer park the miners had to walk to work from neighbouring villages – from Hoyland Common, Pilley, Harley, Wentworth and Thorpe Hesley.

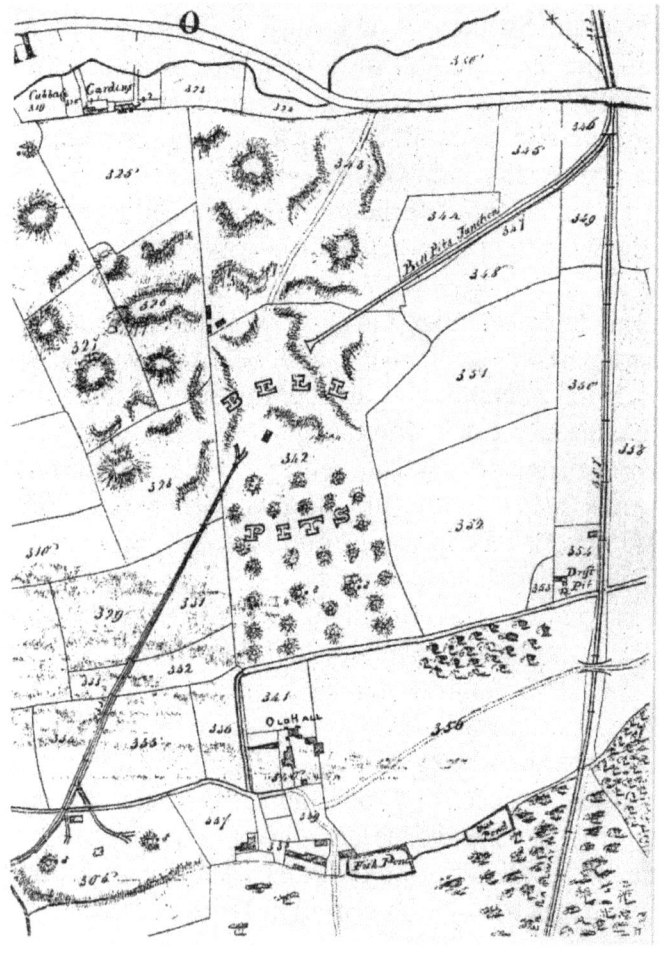

Figure 4. Ironstone bell pits in Tankersley Park. *WWM A-647-14.*

Besides boosting industrial expansion and providing income for the estate the mining of ironstone had a great impact on the park landscape at Tankersley, resulted in population growth and settlement expansion. Tankersley Park was a medieval deer park created in the early fourteenth century and contained about 250 red deer in the 1650s. As ironstone mining expanded in the nineteenth century, the deer were restricted to an ever decreasing area and the herd, then numbering fifty-five red deer, were eventually relocated in Wentworth Park in the 1850s. After the cessation of ironstone mining parts of the park and surrounding area in the first part of the nineteenth century were in parts systematically levelled, and the levelled and un-levelled areas planted with trees (Jones, 1984). In the south of Tankersley parish, beyond the boundary of the deer park, Thorncliffe Wood was doubled in size and to the north of it appeared Newbiggin Plantation. Beyond the park boundary to the north, Potter Holes, Twelve Lands and Tankersley Plantations were created and in the park itself Hood Hill Plantation and Bell Ground came into being. Altogether these plantations covered nearly 280 acres (112 hectares). Bell Ground, a beech plantation established in the 1860s was the wooded area where, Billy Casper, the hero of the book *A Kestrel for a Knave* by Barry Hines, was bird nesting when he saw the kestrel fly from the ruins of the medieval Monastery Farm. The farm was based on the ruins of Tankersley Old Hall which survive in the middle of the former park Significantly the author was the son of a miner and was born and brought up in Hoyland Common.

Many of the Tankersley ironstone miners, especially those working in Tankersley Park and at the deep mine at Skiers Spring lived in nearby Hoyland Common. In 1771 when William Fairbank surveyed Hoyland for the 2nd Marquis of Rockingham, a settlement at Hoyland Common did not exist. There were small holdings at Hoyland Lane End to the east, but Hoyland Common was just that, a common, covering 210 acres (85 hectares) (Jones, 2000). By 1851 a new settlement had been created beside the Wakefield to Sheffield turnpike road which ran in a south-easterly direction along the western edge of the common. In that year the population of Hoyland Common was 195. Of the 71 employed males living there, 39 were miners of whom 34 were ironstone miners. By the end of the nineteenth century Hoyland Common was a large, sprawling industrial village (Figure 5).

Iron Manufacturing

The South Yorkshire estate of the Wentworth- Fitzwilliams was the home of three ironworks established at the end of the eighteenth century, two of which, the Milton Ironworks and Elsecar Ironworks, were closed in the late nineteenth century, and one, Thorncliffe, which continued until the last quarter of the twentieth century. The Milton Ironworks, situated to the south of Hoyland village was established sometime between 1799 and 1802. It was leased by the Walkers of Masbrough, and then by Hartop, Sorby and Littlewood from 1821 to 1824. After Hartop's partners withdrew, Hartop went into partnership with the Graham brothers, London iron merchants who invested £30,000 in the business. Hartop withdrew from the business in 1829 and the Graham brothers operated alone until 1849 when they decided to give up the works.

The nearby Elsecar Ironworks, which was in fact located just over the township boundary in Brampton, was established in 1795. It was leased until 1827 by John Darwin and Co, but from that date until the 1840s it it was run by managers directly on behalf of Earl Fitzwilliam.

When the Graham brothers business failed in 1849, the Earl decided to lease both the Milton and Elsecar Ironworks, and a tenancy agreement was drawn up with George and William Henry Dawes, the sons of John Dawes, the ironmaster who ran the Bromford Ironworks in West Bromwich in the 'Black Country' of Staffordshire. The Dawes brothers brought more than 200 migrant workers with them from the Black Country. At first ironstone supplies for the Dawes' business came from the bell pits in Tankersley Park and from the two deep pits, one in Tankersley Park and the other at Skiers Spring, but from the late 1850s Frodingham ironstone from north Lincolnshire was being 'imported'. George Dawes then set up a new ironworks, the Trent Ironworks in Scunthorpe and in 1884 he gave up the Elsecar and Milton Ironworks, by which time local ironstone mining had come to an end.

Newton Chambers at Thorncliffe Ironworks, established in 1793 on land leased from the Wentworth estate and with their ironstone and coal mined from seams running beneath the estate, have a remarkable history extending into the last quarter of the twentieth century (Jones & Jones, 1993). In the nineteenth century they specialised in making gas lighting plant and gasworks plant. Between 1830 and 1846, for example, they supplied gasworks plant and gas lighting equipment to over 100 towns and cities throughout Britain and Europe. In the second half of the nineteenth century the manufacture of gasworks plant continued to be of major importance and one of the biggest projects was the manufacture of a complete gas works plant for Buenos Aires in Argentina in 1888. The components were shipped to Argentina, erected there and supplied with coal from Newton Chambers pits until the outbreak of the First World War in 1914.

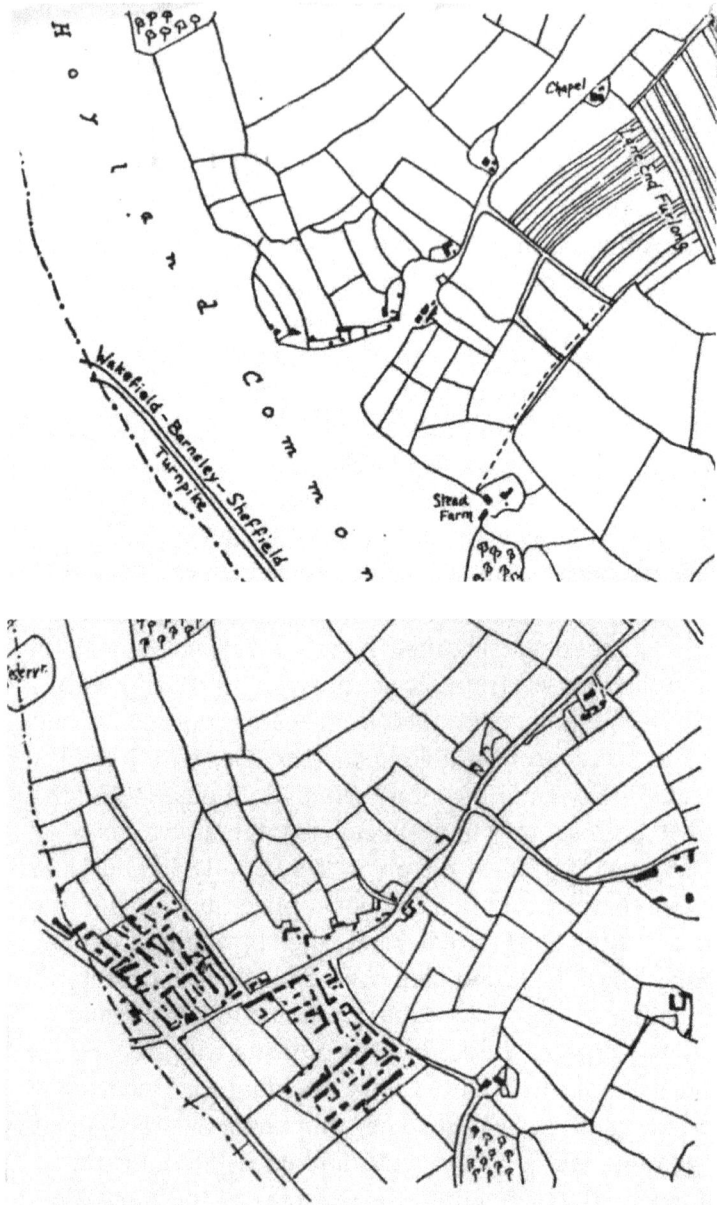

Figure 5: Hoyland Common in 1771 (top) and 1894 (bottom).

Newton Chambers were also famous, of course, as the manufacturers of the disinfectant Izal as a by-product of coke making, and this like their cast iron products soon found an international market. About 1890 Izal was exported to New Zealand as a sheep dip and then was used in the Boer War in base and field hospitals to treat dysentery. And in the early years of the twentieth century agencies were opened in various parts of South Africa, in West Africa, Egypt, Canada, India, Burma, Malaya and even Manchuria.

Coal Mining

Much has been written about coal mining on the Wentworth esstate (e.g. Ward, 1963; Mee, 1975; and Medlicott, 1998). This is hardly surprising so intensively was the coalfield within the estate boundaries exploited. There are records of at least 20 collieries that operated within four miles (six kilometres) of Wentworth Woodhouse in the last 250 years. The first detailed records of coal mining on the Wentworth estate date from the eighteenth century. These relate to Low Wood Colliery and Elsecar Colliery. Low Wood was in Wentworth and Brampton Bierlow townships and Elsecar was just inside Hoyland township less than a mile to the north-east. The first record of Low Wood Colliery is 1723. Elsecar was first mentioned in 1750. Both collieries worked the Barnsley seam near its outcrop, the pits sunk for Elsecar Colliery being no more than 16 yards (15 metres) deep. This seam was nine feet thick. From the early 1750s both collieries were under the estate's direct control. The markets for Elsecar coal were more local than those for Low Wood coal. They stretched north-eastwards into an area where there were no rival collieries, the route crossing the River Dearne towards the magnesian limestone escarpment and the lowlands beyond. The market for Low

Wood coal stretched in the same direction but also included lowland areas further east extending into Nottinghamshire and Lincolnshire. Transport for Elsecar coal was all by horse-drawn wagon but Low Wood coal was transported by cart five miles (eight kilometres) to the estate wharf on the River Don at Kilnhurst where it could be transported on the canalised river to markets on the lower Don and Trent. There was an ulterior motive in selling coal in settlements along the magnesian limestone escarpment. In return a regular supply of limestone was brought to be burnt in the estate lime kilns and then spread on agricultural land on the estate. The bridge over the River Dearne on the wagon route from Elsecar colliery was and still is called Marl or Marle's Bridge.

The presence of the thick Barnsley seam and other seams, principally the Silkstone Seam and the Parkgate Seam, that could be reached from deep pits, together with improving transport links by canal and railway, and the expanding ironworks on the estate, all contributed to the vast expansion of the coal mining industry on the South Yorkshire estate from the late eighteenth century onwards. The first canal development took place in the early 1780s when the Greasbrough Canal was constructed. The canal ran for about one and a half miles from Cinder Bridge where lime kilns were constructed. Waggonways ran from the Greasbrough Colliery (formerly called the Bassingthorpe Colliery) to Cinder Bridge. The canal became redundant in the 1820s and was later filled in except for a short arm to Park Gate Colliery. Park Gate Colliery was a major supplier of coke to the Parkgate Iron & Steel Works.

Within little more than a decade of the opening of the Greasbrough Canal, the Act of Parliament for constructing the Dearne & Dove Canal along nine miles of the Dearne valley, with cuts to Elsecar and Worsbrough, received Parliamentary sanction and the Elsecar branch was completed by 1796 as far as Cobcar Ings. By 1799 it had been extended to Elsecar where a new colliery, Elsecar New Colliery was sunk. The colliery pumping shaft was powered by a Newcomen-type engine which has survived to the present day virtually intact and *in situ* and is a Scheduled Ancient Monument. Not only was there a new colliery at Elsecar but the workings at the old Elsecar Colliery were extended and by 1850 there were three Elsecar collieries: Elsecar High Colliery (the old Elsecar Colliery), Elsecar Mid Colliery (formerly Elsecar New Colliery with a new shaft at Jump) and Elsecar Low Colliery at Hemingfield just inside Wombwell township. Both the Mid Colliery and the shaft of the New Colliery at Jump were connected by inclined planes to the canal. In 1851 all there of these collieries were connected to the railway system when a branch line of the Dearne valley route of the South Yorkshire railway was built to a goods station at Elsecar. They were superseded in 1853 by the sinking of a new colliery, Simon Wood Colliery whose shaft reached the Barnsley seam at 93 yards. This colliery was in production for almost half a century before closing in 1903. It was superseded by Elsecar Main colliery in 1908 designed initially to exploit the Parkgate Seam at 344 yards (Figure 6). Elsecar Main Colliery closed in 1983.

Figure 6: Elsecar Main Colliery. *Old Barnsley*

To the south-east of Wentworth Woodhouse in the Parkgate- Rawmarsh area, besides the Park Gate Colliery, the estate also operated collieries at Stubbin also to supply Parkgate Iron & Steel Works and Park Gate Forge. The early twentieth century survivor was Top Stubbin Colliery that dated from about 1870. It worked the Barnsley Seam but reserves were becoming exhausted by the early years of the twentieth century and the 7th Earl Fitzwilliam decided to open a new colliery to work the six feet thick Parkgate Seam and later also worked the Silkstone Seam. The first sods of No 1 shaft of the New Stubbin Colliery were removed by Lord Milton, the earl's two-year old son in 1913, work on the shafts commenced in 1915 and coal as wound up the shaft for the first time in 1919. The colliery closed in 1978.

All the collieries mentioned so far were worked directly on behalf of the heads of the Wentworth estate. But they also leased mining rights to other companies. One of these was called Vizard's Colliery at Platts Common which came into operation in about 1840. This colliery was deepened and enlarged 1876 and re-named the Hoyland Silkstone Colliery. It worked the Silkstone, Thorncliffe and Parkgate and Flockton seams. Coke was also made at the colliery. It was linked to both the railway and the canal. In 1898 1,260 men and boys worked underground. It closed in 1928 by which time it had been acquired by Newton Chambers & Co. This firm had leased from the Wentworth estate the mineral rights just one and a half miles (two kilometres) to the south-west of Platts Common and opened Rockingham Colliery in 1875 to work the Silkstone and Parkgate seams (Figure 7). Like Hoyland Silkstone, Rockingham had a large number of coke ovens, 170 in all, erected in 1883, which were the main source of the oil by-products of coke making that were converted into the firm's famous disinfectant Izal. From 1930, after the closure of the coke ovens, until 1965 an overhead ropeway four and a half miles (seven kilometres) long, carried the coal from Rockingham Colliery to the coking plant at Smithy Wood.

Figure 7: Rockingham Colliery. *Chapeltown & High Green Archive*

The colliery closed in 1979. Newton Chanbers also leased other coal reserves on the Wentworth estate and had a colliery in Tankersley Park (Tankersley Colliery), Westwood Colliery, Newbiggin Colliery and Thorncliffe Colliery. Thorncliffe Colliery was a drift pit rather than a deep shaft colliery and closed in 1955. They also leased Barley Hole Colliery from the estate, that opened in 1887 and closed in 1975 together with Thorpe Colliery which was sunk between 1900-1903 and closed in 1972. Both of these collieries became service pits for Newton Chambers' Smithywood Colliery. The 4th Earl Fitzwilliam also leased the coal reserves beneath his Tinsley estate which lay next to the Tinsley to Sheffield section of the South Yorkshire Navigation which opened up markets for coal and coke in Sheffield. In the 1840s the lease of Tinsley Park Colliery was obtained by Benjamin Huntsman & Co. At first the coal was obtained from bell pits but in 1852 a deep shaft was sunk. This colliery did not close until 1942. In an outlying part of the Wentworth estate in what is now West Yorkshire, Hemsworth Colliery was sunk in 1894. The colliery merged with South Kirkby Colliery in 1967. South Kirkby Colliery closed in 1988. The village close to the site of Hemsworth Colliery is called Fitzwilliam and was originally a pit village.

Through two centuries the estate earned a considerable amount of money through the direct operation of collieries and through leasing mineral rights to other companies. This of course stopped on the nationalisation of the coal industry by the Labour government in 1947. And although intensively mined, criss-crossed by waggonways and inclined planes, penetrated by the canal and the railway system and dotted with expanding industrial settlements, Wentworth house, garden, park, and indeed most of the township of Wentworth, remained as an island untouched

by the Industrial Revolution ... until 1943. In that that year
and through the following decade this island was gradually
turned upside down by open-cast coal mining on behalf of
the Ministry of Fuel and Power . At first open-cast mining
came to within yards of the great terrace wall bounding the
southern edge of the gardens , and then took place within
the gardens themselves, almost reaching the front door of
the west-facing Baroque frontage. These operations took
place against a background of outrage and protest supported
by the vast majority of the local population who saw the
park and the unindustrialised heart of the estate as one of
the last remaining islands of historic countryside in the
area. In a report in the *Sheffield Telegraph* as early as 1945,
a First World War veteran said the landscape reminded him
of '1917 and the landscape around Paschendaele'. To many
observers the open-cast operations at Wentworth looked
like a personal vendetta by Emanuel Shinwell, the Minister
of Fuel and Power, against Earl Fitzwilliam, a
representative of the old order.

Conclusion

The Wentworth-Fitzwilliams not only provided
employment, but home comforts and health care. They built
houses for their workers, had estate almshouses, gave
pensions to widows and employed doctors to look after the
health of their employees.

At Elsecar, for example, they created an estate industrial
village which survives largely intact to this day, a testament
to the high quality of the housing provided. The oldest
surviving working men's houses at Elsecar are the fifteen
stone cottages that make up Old Row which date from
about 1795. The ten cottages on Station Row were built in
about 1800 probably based on designs by John Carr, the

York architect, who was employed on various schemes at that time by the 4th Earl Fitzwilliam. The largest row at Elsecar is Reform Row, consisting of 28 cottages constructed in 1837 (Figure 8). The two attractive rows that make up Cobcar Terrace were built about 1860. In 1845 the Mines Commissioner, Seymour Tremenheere, described the housing provided for the miners at Elsecar as 'of a class superior in size and arrangement and in the conveniences attached, to those belonging to the working classes.' 'The gardens' he went onto say 'were cultivated with care'. Besides the housing, Elsecar was also provided with Holy Trinity church in 1843 at the expense of the 5th Earl Fitzwilliam and the neighbouring school was built in 1852 to replace an earlier school. The village had street lighting from 1857 and a Market Hall was opened in 1870. And in 1853 even a miners' lodging house was opened that accommodated 22 single men.

Their benevolent attitude to their workers is also well exemplified by their stance with regard to the St Thomas's Day tradition in the nineteenth century. This was on the 21 December, the winter solstice, the shortest day and the longest night of the year. On that day poor people begged money and provisions for Christmas. St Thomas's Day in the nineteenth century was institutionalised on the South Yorkshire Wentworth estate by successive earls Fitzwilliam (Figure 8). There are very full records of the custom throughout the first half of the nineteenth century. For example, in 1841 just over 1,000 servants and employees (except those in the mansion who had separate arrangements) received a gift (WWM A 1412). In the 1840s everyone got sixpence and a quantity of beef. In 1841 the beef distributed amounted to 439 stones (2788 kg). Everyone had to turn up personally and names were ticked off lists drawn up by heads of departments. In 1841 the lists included 631 coal miners (181 at Elsecar New Colliery, 188 at Elsecar Old Colliery, 126 at Parkgate Colliery, 54 at Stubbin Colliery and 55 at Strafford Main), 24 ironstone miners (these were maintenance staff, the miners themselves being regarded as self-employed), 54 ironworkers, 19 woodmen, 43 gardeners, 40 carpenters, 35 masons and even a 'boat tenter' at the lakes in the park, a rat catcher and a bed maker in the stables. And the same list of employees was used in the following March on Collop Monday, which along with Shove Tuesday was traditionally a day of games, dancing and feasts to consume the food forbidden in Lent. On Collop Monday the outdoor employees of Earl Fitzwilliam were given a quantity of beef and bacon.

References

Clayton, A. K. (1973) *Hoyland Nether*, Hoyland Nether Urban District Council.
Jones, M. (1980) 'The Mapping of Unconsidered Trifles: A Yorkshire Example', *The Local Historian*, Volume 14, Number 3, 156-163.
Jones, M. (1984) 'Woodland Origins in a South Yorkshire Parish', *The Local Historian*, Volume 16, Number 2, 73-82.
Jones, M. (1986) 'Coppice Wood Management in the Eighteenth Century: an example from County Wicklow', *Irish Forestry*, Volume 43, No1, 15-31.
Jones, M. (1988) 'Combining Estate records with Census Enumerators' Books to Study Nineteeth Century Communities: The Case of the Tankersley Ironstone Miners *c*. 1850', *Local Population Studies,* No. 41, Autumn, 1988, 13-27.
Jones, M. (1995) 'Ironstone Mining at Tankersley in the Nineteenth Century for Elsecar and Milton Ironworks', in

B. Elliott (ed) *Aspects of Barnsley: Discovering Local History, Volume 3*, Wharncliffe Publishing Ltd, 80-115.
Jones, M. (2000) *The Making of the South Yorkshire Landscape*, Wharncliffe Books.
Jones, J. and Jones, M. (1993) *'....A Most Enterprising Thing...': an illustrated history of Newton Chambers*, Chapeltown & High Green Archive.
Jones, M. and Walker, P. (1997) 'From Coppice-with-standards to High Forest: the Management of Ecclesall Woods 1715-1901', *The Natural History of Ecclesall Woods, Part 1, Peak District Journal of Natural History and Archaeology,* Special Publication No 1, July 1997, 11-20.
Medlicott, I. (1998) 'Coal Mining on the Wentworth Estate 1740-1840' in M. Jones (ed) *Aspects of Rotherham: Discovering Local History, Volume 3*, Wharncliffe Publishing Ltd, pp. 135-152.
Mee, G. (1975) *Aristocratic Enterprise; The Fitzwilliam Industrial Undertakings 1795-1857*, Blackie and Son Ltd.
Tremenheere, S. (1845) *Report on the Mining Population in parts of Scotland and Yorkshire.*

Figure 8: Reform Row, Elsecar.

Snuff and Grouse: The Wilsons of Sharrow

David Hey

The Sharrow Snuff Mills within the ancient parish of Sheffield were established on the Porter Brook in the mid eighteenth century on the site of a former cutler's grinding wheel. The snuff business flourishes to this day in a surprisingly secluded setting amidst rows of Victorian housing. The Georgian house, mill and dam survive and the water wheel can still be turned for visitors.

Figure 1: The Sharrow Snuff Mill.

In 1738 Thomas Wilson, a shearsmith, leased the site, but the first record of a snuff mill is from 1763, when Thomas's son, Joseph, who had been trained as a silversmith, was in charge. Two previous snuff mills had been erected on Sheffield's rivers: in 1749 on the Storrs Brook, a tributary of the River Loxley, and a decade later at Owlerton.[1] This new business arose after Thomas Boulsover's invention of Old Sheffield Plate in 1742. Joseph Wilson and Boulsover became partners and one of their ventures was the manufacture of snuff boxes, for it was a logical and profitable development to grind the snuff that went into these metal containers.

Joseph's grandsons, William Wilson (1799-1887) and George Wilson (1802-1878) improved the family's fortunes considerably by successful investments as shareholders in several local businesses. Their leisure time was taken up by fox hunting and game shooting in the countryside to the west of Sheffield, so much so that these pursuits eventually displaced almost all their other interests and the resources of the two branches of the family. In 1860 George Wilson bought Derwent Moor and, four years later, he added the adjoining Moscar Moor, both prime grouse-shooting areas since the parliamentary enclosure of these moors in the early nineteenth century.[2]

This was the time when the shooting of grouse was altered radically by the invention of the breach-loading shot gun and the construction of lines of shooting butts. In the past, birds had been shot as they flew away, but now beaters were employed to drive the birds towards the 'sportsmen'. By the 1880s the bags of grouse that were shot each day in the shooting season were enormous. The moors were managed solely for the rearing and shooting of grouse. The heather was burnt on a rotation basis to encourage new growth while preserving some cover against predators; shooting cabins were built; and drains were cut in the wettest parts.[3]

The next generation of Wilsons were amongst the most prominent moor owners in the late-Victorian and Edwardian hey-day of grouse shooting: William Wilson of Beauchief Hall (1850-1927) and his cousin, George Kingsford Wilson of Ecclesall (1853-1933). William's primary interest, at first, was fox hunting. In 1878 he became Master of the Barlow Hunt and he built the kennels that are still in use at Horsleygate, but in 1900 he suffered a spinal injury in a hunting accident and so he turned solely to shooting grouse.

Figure 2. William Wilson (1850-1927), standing, with his father and son.

Three years earlier, he had bought the Duke of Norfolk's estate of over 2,000 acres on the Stanage and Hallam moors, together with the lodge that had been erected in the middle of them in 1869. The sale was advertised as 'The Finest Sporting Estate ever offered in Sheffield or District'. About the same time, another industrialist, Wilson Mappin, the younger son of Sir Frederick Mappin, the owner of the Queen's Cutlery Works, purchased the moor that extends from the Stanage escarpment to Bamford Edge. Eleven stones, inscribed WW on one side and WM on the other, still mark the boundary between these moorland estates. [4]

Figure 3: A typical grouse drinking trough, the first of the third set, starting in Oaking Clough.

In 1907 William Wilson began an extraordinary project that is of interest to the landscape historian and archaeologist and to the numerous ramblers who now have access to these moors. In the next few years he ordered the construction of 108 artificial drinking troughs in the natural boulders of his moor, so that his grouse would not fly away and be shot on someone else's estate. Barrie Blanksby and I have mapped 103 of these, but we were unable to find the other five, which appear to have literally sunk without trace in the peat. Our project took a few years to complete because some of the troughs were well hidden in the heather and we had to wait until it was burnt in the rotation cycle.

Figure 4: Number 25 in the third set was not discovered until the heather was burnt.

A typical trough is about 18 inches long and 12 inches wide but some are much larger and the styles are varied. Wilson's idea seems to have come from similar basins that were formed naturally through the swirling action of the wind and the rain. Rainwater flowed into the troughs along runnels, which were cut to fit the shape of the rock. The troughs are not arranged in a regular manner, for some are close together while others are up to 400 yards apart. Nor are they in a line, for they zig-zag in and out of the moors. Each trough is numbered in one of three sequences.

An account book reveals that a teenage mason, George Broomhead was paid 7s.3$^{1}/_{2}$d. per trough. Carving the troughs seems to have been his apprenticeship work. His first stone near Stanage Pole has two long runnels leading the rainwater down to the basin and is inscribed, 'W. Wilson / 1907 / No 1'. This first group of six troughs is not well known because it is now difficult to access.

Figure 5. The first of the 108 grouse drinking troughs, near Stanage Pole.

The success of the first venture encouraged Wilson to undertake a much more ambitious scheme of 75 troughs that stretch along Stanage Edge before curving back into the moor. The troughs on the Stanage escarpment are the ones that are well known to the public, but most walkers have no idea that these form less than a third of the total. A third erratic line of 27 troughs begins at Oaking Clough, near the northern boundary of Wilson's moor and descends to Wyming Brook. Some of these troughs have ingenious designs, including two that were cut into the vertical face of the rock. Together, the troughs are a unique feature in the Peak District, for Wilson's idea was not taken up by any other owner.

Figure 6: Number 13 in the third set is vertical instead of horizontal.

Notes

[1] C. Ball, D. Crossley and N. Flavell, eds, *Water Power on the Sheffield Rivers* (second, revised edition; Sheffield: South Yorkshire Industrial History Society, 2006), pp. xvi, xxi, 50, 60, 74, 114 and 135.

[2] M.H.F. Chaytor, *The Wilsons of Sharrow: The Snuff-Makers of Sheffield* (Sheffield: Northend, 1962), p. 160.

3. D. Hey, 'The Grouse Moors of the Peak District', in P.S. Barnwell and M. Palmer, eds, *Post-Medieval Landscapes: Landscape History after Hoskins*, 3 (2007), pp. 68-79; D. Hey, *A History of the Peak District Moors* (Barnsley: Pen & Sword, 2014).

4. D. Hey, *Historic Hallamshire* (Ashbourne: Landmark, 2002), pp. 95-111.

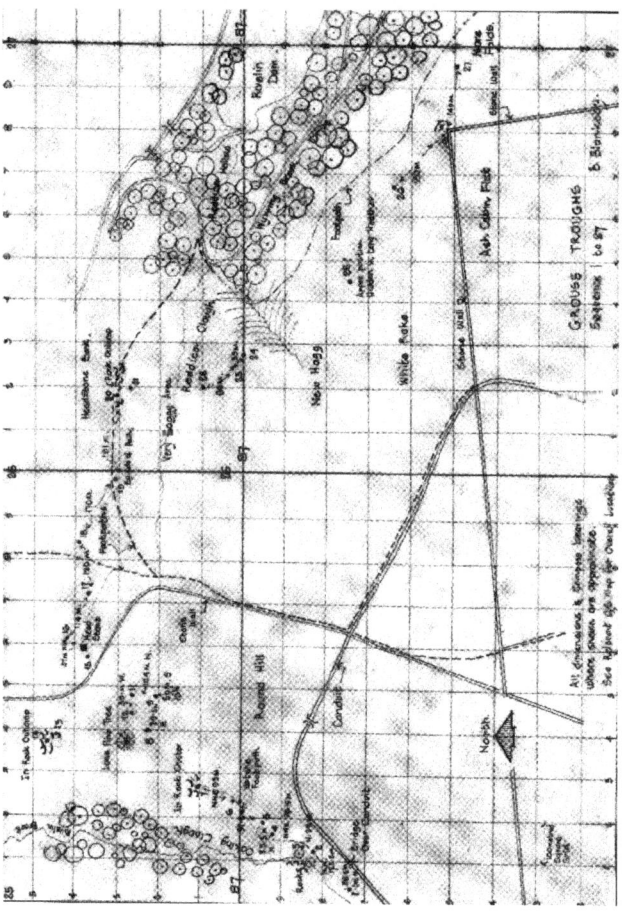

Figure 7. Barrie Blanksby's map of the 27 troughs in the third set.

PLACE (People, Landscape & Cultural Environment of Yorkshire) www.place.uk.com

The PLACE Education & Research Centre has been an independent charity since 2004. PLACE has a virtual office based at York St John University in York, and is governed by a Board of Directors. The Chief Executive is Dr Margaret Atherden.
PLACE is a registered charity (no. 1106814) and a company limited by guarantee (registered no. 5086325). Place has the following charitable objects:
- To promote research into the people, landscape and cultural environment of Yorkshire and elsewhere and to disseminate the useful results for the benefit of the general public.
- To advance the education of the public in the people and the natural and cultural heritage of Yorkshire and elsewhere.

South Yorkshire Biodiversity Research Group (S. Yorks Econet) www.ukeconet.org

South Yorkshire Biodiversity Research Group is a fully constituted, non-for-profit, voluntary organisation established in the 1990's. The Group organise, run, and deliver community-based, citizen science training throughout South Yorkshire and also nationally, in partnership with major universities and other key stakeholders. Our work involves: a) Connecting people with nature; b) work with lesser known plants, animals and organisms; and also, c) raising awareness of large-scale conservation of natural environments on land to help counter the effects of damaging human activities. (The latter are achieved in partnership with major projects on re-wetting the Humberhead Levels, on restoring the Pennine peat bogs and moors, and through our research work on 're-constructing nature', and on 'wilding' the landscape).

South Yorkshire Biodiversity Research Group provides a forum for the dissemination of information on biodiversity, landscape and environmental conservation issues. We work with a broad range of stakeholder groups, individuals, schools and colleges, including hard-to-reach groups within the community.